When a MAN LOVES a WOMAN

ALFRED L. CALVERT

WHEN A MAN LOVES A WOMAN
Copyright © 2004 Alfred L. Calvert

Alfred L. Calvert
P. O. Box 105
Keego Harbor, MI 48320
(248) 259-6998
alcalvert45@gmail.com

All rights No part of this publication may be reproduced, stored in a retrieval system, or transmitted in any form by means of electronic, mechanical, photo-copying, recording, or otherwise, except for the inclusion of brief quotations in a review, without prior permission in writing from the author and publisher.

Book Design by Shannon Crowley
Treasure Image & Publishing - TreasureImagePublishing.com

Dedication

I, Alfred L. Calvert proudly dedicate this book to my wife Vikki Calvert who proves daily that unconditional love is possible and her dedication is the substratum for love and marriage. And to my wonderful daughter Kim Calvert Lehman, and son Alfred Jr., who loves their dad unconditionally regardless of my physical challenges and very sordid past life.

I applaud you who have not given up in your relationships/marriage struggles; and admonish you to never allow anyone to excoriate you for forgiving and forgetting the past to move forward into the future.

Introduction

There are no stronger forces, no greater spirit on planet earth than love. Everybody need it and can't live without it. People have killed because of it.

Kingdoms have been toppled and queens have left their kings because they did not get it. Many have committed suicide because they never felt it; others have gone insane because someone else did not show it.

We surrender to rigorous exercise, surgery and dieting because of our search for it. Some live and die never finding it. Some spend their lives trying to buy it.

However, in all that we do to capture and acquire it, love is free; it will always conquer hate, you are free to love.

So, you just ought to love that woman.

Preface

Our purpose here is to help you who are somewhat struggling in your relationships. This book is to teach man to love his woman unconditionally and the art of making love, to always alleviate acrimony from the relationship.

Let's be very clear, sex and marriage is right per moral law, but people choose their own antinomian of this principal. However, inside or outside of our faith married or un- married we all need love and is prone by human nature to have sex to find it, people desire love and sex.

Sexual relationships are just as much a part of life for you as it is for others; even creatures of the planet have sex. However, it is the one virtue that have gotten us all in trouble with some regrets. On the other hand, some have found great felicity in loving relationships.

Hopefully this book will help to save your relationship or marriage, especially those of you who will love each other unconditionally.

Footnote

My advice to all; if you desire to keep your relationship, work on it daily.

You, empty trash out of your home once a week, empty trash out of your family life every day and love each other unconditionally.

Table of Contents

Dedication 3
Introduction 5
Preface 7

SHE IS...

(Prologue) 11

ONE

RIB BONE meat gone SUCK ON 15
Bone almost gone, Suck on! 24
Love is a Wonderful Thang 30

TWO

Bone Dry On the Outside, Wet On the Inside 47
Don't Take Her for Granted! 51
I'm Woman Who Needs Sexual Healing 61
Good Girls Gone Wild 64
Negative Turns Positive 69
Grow Up So You Can Catch Up! 72
It Was There All The Time! 76

THREE

Obsession or Depression 81
Mystery Unfolded 89
Women Love Power and Purpose! 94

The Duty of Man! 103
Marriage a la Carte' 109
I Was Made To Love Her 119

FOUR

Lose Your Manhood, Lose Your Woman! 141
Women Are Wiser Than You Think! 145
No Fun When The Rabbit Gets The Gun! 146
Unauthorized Liberation 154
The Serious Doctor Examines The Whole Body 172

FIVE

Some Bones to Suck On 181

SIX

Variety of Bones to Suck On! 207

She is...

(Prologue)

The American woman is the most liberated, intelligent, glamorous lady on planet earth; it is from her we received our birth.

She is exposed to financial freedom, freedom of speech, freedom of religion, movie stars; show bars.

She is frequently shopping for designer shoes, St John Knits, she is educated her life is upgraded. Her shoulder decorated with Gucci, Coach, and Louie, Tory Burch, she loves hard, drives luxury cars.

When unexpected she flirts, when she shouldn't she smirks, she will she won't; when she should she don't.

Don't take her for granted, on shaky ground she won't be planted. She is in school; she is no fool; her credit is tight she's all right.

She loves long walks, long talks, she births, she hurts, she bleeds and she haves needs.

When she can, she will, when she does she thrills, she lends, she spends, she looks, and she cooks.

She blesses, she messes, she dances, she romances, she is the mother of all living, and she is forgiving.

She shops, she flops she is insecure but will endure, she stretches and she confesses.

She lies, she cries, she cares, she shares, in some cases she is single and love to mingle.

She is plump, she is tall, she is slim, she is small, she opens, she shuts down, she smiles, and she frowns. She is bitter, she is sweet, bad hair day, next day she is neat, she is attentive, she is aloof, she is tight, and she is loose.

Prologue

She is good, she is bad, she is happy she is sad, she fusses, she cusses, she swears, and she dares.

She is rich she is poor; of everything she is and is not there is one thing for sure as heaven above… she needs your unconditional love.

One

RIB BONE MEAT GONE SUCK ON

Do not let her go yet!

The dash between the two dates separating birth and death on planet earth is to be lived, enjoyed to the fullest and not understood.

For us to understand life we would have to understand the cosmological origin of outer space and structure of the universe, mountains, hills, rivers, forest and seas, the fullness of the creator's providential purpose and epistemologically have facts concerning human limitations and exact knowledge of the creator's omnipotence, omniscience, and Omni-presence.

There would be no need for epistemological discussions, or any ontological argument concerning the existence of God, the finite would have no need for the infinite.

It is a mystery how the first anesthesia was applied to man who fell in deep sleep and part of his rib bone was taken and the womb mysteriously closed, but man's heart, passions, emotions and sensuality remained open to the rib bone made into a woman who was never told to work or succumb to any stress, but to be an ambience in the garden to remain beautiful, as the essence of femininity, the personification of female, the embodiment of sheism; woman is the help meet to man, one who is suitable for man — the only conscious being who has the capacity to naturally satisfy man.

Even in the curse she was told to travail in child birth but never a word intimating she is not to be loved and cared for. In fact, if we consider the splendor of the Garden of Eden which was her home, everything was provided, and she was ultimately created to remain aesthetically in her pulchritudinous splendor and loved extravagantly.

If we understood all the mysteries of life, we would never look outside of ourselves for help and could predict the times of our failures and successes along with the ambiguous chagrin from the vicissitudes of life which we all should know by now is impossible.

I'm persuaded that someone somewhere longs for all of us to appreciate Him for everything done whether big or small. In his infinite wisdom, he has allowed even the tragedies of life to smart us.

"Failures in life are not stop signs, but road maps to continued success." Robert Shuler

Have you ever considered who aberrated the path we were on; orchestrated a new course for our good and out of all the others on planet earth made sure that we meet a special someone, fall in love and never have the desire to lose them?

Everyone born into the colony of time on planet earth has encountered a friendly physical attraction with someone whether it was in passing, a one-night stand, a secret lover or lasting relationship.

Often times, we realize later in life that we should have applied more energy toward the one who got away, instead of wasting our lives with the one who got in the way and lead our lives into the abyss of nowhere.

There are some one-night stands that bring back fond memories, and there are memories of childhood sweethearts who were so very exciting, especially the high school romance that we thought would never end, but the stratification process and vicissitudes of life in most cases dealt us another hand.

There is no greater pleasure, moments of ecstasy, no greater depths of desire, no touch, no feeling, no emotion and no passion, greater than the amalgamation between man and woman who were attracted to each other, eventually became lovers; who's contradistinction only enhanced the romance to the realization they were meant for each other and came together as lovers and the best of friends.

They bonded, sexually, spiritually, and intellectually knowing that without a doubt they would enjoy each other despite each other's short comings, faults and a willingness to forsake all others; never losing the novelty of their loves, and never capturing copiously the apex of their bonding together, but always striving to become one with each other.

*Come unite with me with an open mind, with a heart full of love and let's enjoy each other in the now with anticipation of being together again tomorrow **and forever.***

The heated passion between man and woman who became lovers, firstly became friends is the most passionate, uncontrollable, fulfilling desire filled with loveable emotions.

You cannot explain it, or plan it, in the absence of it; you feel you cannot live without it and you won't ever forget about it, life seems hopeless and useless without it.

Without unconditional love, life would be a mistake.

It is unconditional, passionate love, when friends love each other's shortcomings, can look beyond each other faults and see their needs. It is here where it becomes difficult to even sit next to each other without the sexual appetite arousing sensual hunger to its pentacle of sexual satisfaction; you can call it lust or freaky but it is the most pleasurable experience between two human beings.

I want your love, I need your love.

It is the pertinacious position of the writer that if you can find anything on planet earth that causes a man to feel completeness and total satisfaction other than the affections of a woman and her lovingkindness to him, then please share it with us so that we can stop wasting our time looking for it.

The woman is the only suitable conscious being that's naturally appropriated and flexible enough so that man fit perfectly inside of her.

When your lips met mine, I knew you belong to me and we were a perfect match for a lifetime.

She is thoroughly equipped with every appeal, intellect, emotion, passion, touch and the vaginal muscle, that a man need for sexual healing.

Chapter One

"She makes man feel so fine and relieves his mind."
Marvin Gaye

Her value to him is worth the man painstakingly acquiescing to her, overlooking shortcomings with patience, waiting on her for pleasure, searching for her inner most passions, seeking after her warmth and kindness, sacrificing on behalf of her security, put your Mack down to catch and capture her mind, use every moral effort to acquire sustenance for care, securing her life.

"I am woman and God made me for man, there is no one anywhere as unique as I am"

Man should always patiently and painstakingly, create a spiritual and natural atmosphere of comfort for the woman's consciousness to relax her body in the presence of his loves.

Even when the natural atmosphere is dark, her passions are illuminated not only with the light of scented candles including aphrodisiacal arousals for an atmosphere for lovemaking, but also with the expectancy of unconditional love.

In other words, whatever we do in this boudoir (bedroom) stays in the room.

Though you are spiritual; there is nothing spiritual about the act of sexual intercourse, it is all filled with lust and uncontrolled passion between lovers who will enjoy each other enveloping themselves in total ecstasy.

It is very aggravating to hear people say they made love in the spirit, how in the heck is that done; when talking dirty, spanking, oral sex, moaning and screaming together with organisms? God grants us that pleasure in our quality time.

I need to be loved, I must feel special to enjoy my time of being conversant with you, and I must feel secure in your embrace in this place in space and time.

It's necessary to create the proper conditions for love assurance for the woman and is a pleasure to do it, when a man loves a woman.

Chapter One

This assurance must be culminated with the utmost patience, words of comfort because you may never know the sexual experiences she encountered in life that was egregiously painful to the early beginnings of her life.

Someone said that love conquers all. This being the case, it is incumbent upon the lover to consistently work at his craft of building her up with the strongest tool in the box, unconditional love.

Abraham Maslow says, *"if the only tool you have is a hammer, you tend to see every problem as a nail."*

It's always roses, because you may never know the pain, the problems, the conditions she has had to endure before you arrived. Be her knight in shining armor, her hero, her superman.

Rescue her from the frivolities of the world, the pain, scars, vestiges imposed on her from others who were insensitive and took advantage of her vulnerability. Do it man!

Bone almost gone, Suck on!

Take a licking and keep on ticking.

Top 10 signs something is wrong in your marriage:

1. Your wife is in the basement more than the bedroom.
2. Your food is always cold.
3. Your wife shops for eight hours.
4. For the first time this year her nails and feet are manicured.
5. She begins to accuse you of something that happened 10 years ago.
6. Her daily conversation is you get on my nerves.
7. She takes out an insurance policy on you for $1 million.
8. She begins to read books all night long.
9. She wears Bloomers out of the house but come back in thongs.
10. She calls you Johnny and your name is Ray.

Chapter One

Due to a News Week Magazine report 40% of the nation's housewives have cheated on their husbands and an independent study shows that a 60% rate of women has done the same to their lovers.

It becomes critical for the men to find out why?

Why would a woman or lady who was so loving and kind in courtship; who patiently picked six of her most beautiful and trusted friends; matched them with bridegrooms to plan an extravagant wedding; so suddenly cause a lifetime relationship to become ephemeral?

We need one reason why this female, this embodiment of sheism; this essence of femininity, this personification of female who in courtship became a ball of uncontrollable heat of passion that overwhelmed and culminated all of man's desire for her, now is out of control and her lustful passions are in the arms of another.

Her feelings for you was so overwhelming when she exposed her thongs that delineated a message to every sensational fiber of your sexual desire saying come and do what you want to do to me. Now she suddenly began wearing bugs bunny pajamas that sends a definitive message, stay away from me.

Why suddenly would this woman after walking down the isles in tears to Mr. Big stuff, my big daddy, my hunk of love and vowed before God, family and friends to love and obey till death do us part; now have become recalcitrant and in opposition to every vow made, she has now acquiesced her time and attention to the club with male dancers?

What happens in the next six months to a year that causes a couple who talked on the phone all night to suddenly not communicate at all?

Two people, who just a few months earlier; when thoughts of touching each other caused a passionate explosion that erupted into sensual fire, that should have burned in their hearts forever; has now fissile into a spark without hope of ever becoming a flame.

Chapter One

Don't you remember the hours of mouth-to-mouth resuckitation *(made up word)* or should I say sweet suffocation; the all-night tongue kissing, never missing one drop of each other's saliva?

Can't you just one more time pull your panties to the side to the finger fondling and foreplay?

I've gotten use to the lips, hips, and fingertips of you baby that caused each of our bodies to reel out of control until the two of us met as one; in complete conversant sexual communication. This sexual communication is so unimaginable we must seek a higher power for the answers of how to restore our love.

> *"The wife hath not power over her body, but the husband; and likewise, also the husband hath not power of his own body but the wife."*
> *1 Corinthians 7:4*

OOOOH, so this is it, we were created to love extravagantly!

We know it as doing the wild thing or getting busy. We are supposed to rid ourselves of all inhibitions, lose ourselves in each other, in ecstasy, giving all we have passionately to each other holding back nothing; do not fight the power. #boom

So, you are not some freak of nature because you like what you like when you like it.

We must appreciate the natural scent of each other which served as an enticing aroma, an aphrodisiac that lead to inestimable love for each other in heated passion and lovemaking. Take charge and don't allow this pleasure to become stench in each other's nostrils to the point that we sleep in different rooms, lets fix that today!

We must rekindle our relationship and excitement that brought us together; there is no need for a strange judge to hear our situation and affairs dividing everything we materialistically accumulated.

We have the power to help us get better and not bitter, that the spiritual, social and psychological aspect of our lives connect again.

Chapter One

I am your man I can do this because of my love for you.

What and who crept into this blissful life; this home of love making and marital bliss that vowed till death do us part; who imposed the negative sounds of the trumpet to divide us, depart from me, he is a liar, I'm cleaning up my house, kicking the negative out!

I dropped the ball but it has bounced back in my court, and I'm playing this game to win! I know the negative influence; the creator is not the author of our confusion!

Lovers living life together is like protecting two large plots of territory, when you don't continually take or protect the territory, it will overtake you. It's like neglecting the weeds in a beautiful flower garden, if we don't pull the weeds they overtake the garden with ugliness and choke the flowers.

The remedy for overcoming negative obstacles is to conclude that the two of you are better than one, when one fall you have your soul mate to help you up. Two pieces of rope tied together is stronger than one piece, stay together as one. And never go to bed with conversation of acrimony, but let your conversation be filled with the delineation of love and happiness.

No relationship is exempt from problems in life. Life is the only force that begs us to live every second of the 24-hour day, and at any time it has the propensity to knock you down and will keep you down if you don't fight to get backup.

"Getting knocked down in life is a given... getting up and moving forward is a choice." Zig Zigler

"It's not the load that breaks you down, it's the way you carry it." Lena Horne

LOVE IS A WONDERFUL THANG

We can overcome the negative, allow the process of disambiguation's and pass problems to resolve itself; renew our vows and think on things that are true, just and lovely that firstly brought us together.

Chapter One

Let's Forget The Dumb Stuff!

It is true that from the beginning the higher power must have had us in mind to meet and greet each other. Out of all the people in this world we were attracted to each other as one.

If we did not do this ourselves then who did?

It was so natural and justified that I over looked your faults and saw how much you need me and I need you. How lovely that feeling became, how great the admiration for you grew after spending quality time with you.

It's human nature for the novelty of a relationship to diminish just on general principal. However, to counter this, always apply unconditional love.

Sometimes fellows reflect on the time her mother shared her photos as a little girl, the innocence, and how her dad never spent time with her as a child which caused her insecurities.

Have compassion, considering her past, look beyond the faults and pain that the Vicissitudes of life has dealt her. Do you have the heart of mercy to move from the past into the future with her?

"The farthest distance in the world is yesterday."

"Only those who will risk going too far can possibly find out how far one can go." T.S. Eliot

Think of her fragile body, little clumsy ways and how she needs you for strength, and has very little direction without your guidance.

Consider the many times she was unsure of herself and how she model before you in a certain dress and needed your opinion before she purchased it. Think of the many times she prepared the meal of your choice so that she would be pleasing to you outside of the bedroom.

What about the many days and nights she gave of herself unselfishly so that you could just release yourself?

The times when there was no love making on your part but just to get off to satisfy your selfish desires, she succumbed to being every woman at your demand.

Even though she was tired, she came out of her space to fulfill yours.

Why leave this girl to the wolves in the world waiting to devour her of all her innocence and idealistic dreams of ever becoming a better woman or the wonderful human being that her creator intended her to be?

*I'm just a woman that needs a man in
my life to help me!*

I gave myself to you, I'm valuable to you; lets rekindle the love we had in the beginning of our relationship? I need you to help me and not hurt me.

The distance between eleven o'clock and twelve o'clock is the same distance between twelve and one o'clock. Why not go forward instead of backwards? It is the same distance and it takes less effort most of the time to forget about the past and go forward to the future.

If you want something bad enough you will go out and fight for it, work day and night for it.

Simply go after this gift that is only found in the pulchritudinous splendor of the female gender. Simple go after her with all tenacity, in your capacity and sagacity.

If you will bet on her, plan a great life for her, lose all your terror of the opposition to get her, began to dream and scheme about capturing her, humble yourself and realize life is useless without her, you will ultimately win her.

It is true that sometimes we must stop so that we can go, or we must back up so that we can go forward, but when it's a classic it's worth repairing; and a wise man never throws a classic away.

Eight is a new beginning; the creator saved Noah and eight souls to begin replenishing the earth after it was destroyed by a flood.

A negative flood is trying to infiltrate and destroy your relationship. It's time for a new beginning.

Repeat together eight times for eight days:

- *"I can do all things through my creative power who strengthens me..."*
- *"We are more than conquerors together through the creator that loves us."*
- *"When the infinite power is for us who can be against us?"*

You will find reprieve and soothing through these powerful words of life when repeated with the right attitude; and when you add an atmosphere of faith, determination and confidence to them. Your reward will be greater than you can ever ask or think.

There is a power in you that come with how you think, especially when you see the blessings that the infinite power has for your union. Place God in the right mental frame daily in the relationship and you will find deliverance from any negative aspect of your relationship because there is nothing negative concerning your creator.

The more the finite connects with the infinite, the more strength and stability life becomes; and directs life toward perfection.

Once the two of you realize the need for each other, humility creates the foundation for growth in your relationship and causes a greater need for unity and attitude of love for each other. Humility abrogates pride and allows grace which is forgiveness, peace, love and tranquility to abound in every aspect of your lives.

The infinite power of all the universe have placed certain characteristics in us allowing us to instinctively know when to humble ourselves to a certain situation or condition, it reminds us, "you don't miss your water until your well runs dry.

The Serenity Prayer

God grant me the serenity to accept the things I cannot change, the courage to change the things I can, and wisdom to know the difference.

Attitude has much to do with the altitude of our lives. Grace which consist of love, forgiveness, concern, patience are virtues that causes the recipient of a morning bad breath to seek a stronger mouthwash or bad smelling feet after your gym workout to seek stronger foot powder for each other.

Chapter One

The same day that you alleviate all negative thoughts that others have instituted into your mind concerning your life and don't give them any more thoughts than they deserve is the same day a positive seed will take root in your relationship and began to blossom into the beauty that your creative power intended for it to be.

The cultivation of the garden of your mind is a timeless and eternal art, it takes patience to garden the mind of a woman who just may have been molested, by some relative or past relationship.

It is at that time the man must become the master horticulturists.

Nothing can come from the seed of pain, but pain itself, then realizing this fact, why compound pain on top of pain from sometimes childhood vestiges and scars when you have the cure for her pain called unconditional love that looks beyond all her faults and see her needs.

James Allen says, *"As a being of power, Intelligence, love, and the lord of his own thoughts, man holds the key to every situation, and contains within himself that transforming and regenerative agency by which he may make himself what he wills."*

Mister you have the power within you to will a great life for you and the woman, *"When a man loves a woman"*.

Just as a gardener cultivates his plot, keeping it free from weeds, and growing the flowers and fruits which he requires, so may a man tend the garden of his mind, weeding out all the wrong, useless impure thoughts and cultivating toward perfection the flowers and fruits of clear useful pure thoughts.

By doing this, you will discover you are the master gardener of your soul, which encompasses thoughts of beautiful flowers and fruits of love, peace and prosperity for your family and especially she who has the only natural muscle that can ultimately satisfy you. *You certainly want to keep her peaceful.*

Allow me to further extrapolate from a great mind born (1864 - 1912, James Allen), *"the mind is the master weaver, both inner garment of character and the outer garment of circumstance, and that as they may have been woven in ignorance and pain they may now weave in happiness."*

In other words, don't allow the conditions around you to control you but from within with perseverance and determination control the conditions.

The same day you realize you are created for greatness, no matter what state the relationship is in; your heavenly father can bring you out victoriously.

Get up from where you are and tell all foreign voices, back up buster, no weapon formed against us shall prosper, and every tongue that has spoken against us nothing, because I have a power in me that is much greater than you can think.

> *"Greater is he that's in me than anything in the world."*

These positive words of truth and power will abrogate all negativity, weaknesses and lies the enemy has craftily inserted into the relationship, and lead you on a course of hope against hope.

You must keep hope alive.

Why can't we pick up the phone and say I'm sorry, forgive me and help me to be a better person to you?

Pray to God who made us, who brought us together to bless us instead of cursing ourselves and cussing at each other?

The time and frustration it takes to drive across town to hire a lawyer to break up, we should use that time energy and money on a vacation to try and make up, (mend the brokenness).

No situation is hopeless if we are alive in hope. How do we mend the brokenness?

Go to the root cause of what went wrong, forgive myself and ask for forgiveness with the proclivity to never allow it in our space of unity and unconditional love again.

Vacation = vacate our bodies, hearts and minds form all negativity to a place suitable for reconciliation.

Don't allow the outside conditions to control your life but control the condition your life is in; from the inside out.

Oftentimes we expect somethings (substances, therapist, and advice from friends) to change our condition or situation, when it is us that have the capacity to make the change. (Renew the Mind).

Men are anxious to improve their circumstances, but unwilling to improve themselves, we therefore remain bound in pride and selfishness and place ourselves in the unnecessary dog house of love, causing ambiguous thoughts concerning you and your queen, doubting if you are the real king or should she look for another.

A trashed mind will play trashed tricks on you.

Our geographical location does not change our nature. It is what it is; where ever you are does not change who you are.

We can leave town but we cannot leave ourselves, change must begin on the inside.

It is a good time for everyone involved to lay down their ego's which often than not are destructive; and come together with openness and forgiveness. Lay aside every weight that is dragging your emotions down, forget those things in the past and appreciate the now. Savor the moment you are together and look for a better tomorrow.

The ball must hit the floor before it can bounce back up. It may be too heavy for you to hold on to right now. Let go so that it can bounce back by itself.

Don't allow it to pull you down to the floor with it. Let go of fears and negative thoughts they are too heavy. Allow patience to have her perfect work.

Chapter One

Let go of heavy negative emotions that are weighing you down. No one is perfect. Confession is good for the soul, yes, I made some mistakes, and yes, I hurt you, please forgive me and let us pray that our tomorrow is better than our yesterday. "NEVER CONFESS YOU SLEPT WITH ANOTHER WOMAN!!!" NEVA!! NEVA!!!!That is the confession of a fool, not a man!

Believe it or not Prayer does change things!

Pride is antithetical to faith and hinders two people from coming together forgetting those things behind. Pride destroys the fire in the love and the lovemaking.

The wisest man that ever lived under the canopy of heaven says, *"Pride goeth before destruction and a haughty spirit before a fall."*

Too much pride in any relationship or circumstance has already gone before the relationship to destroy it. Check out all the movie stars and famous entertainers who seem to have everything but cannot maintain the main thing; stay together. Egos and too much pride will destroy any relationship.

Good character can lift lives up and bad character can bring it back down.

So many people in or out of stardom cannot remain together because of pride. We can lovingly ingratiate each other, but one side is giving and the other is to prideful to bend. Therefore, the whole thing crumbles.

The stars certainly have the money and the prestige to go anywhere and do everything to mend that which is broken. But pride allows precious broken pieces of the heart mind and soul to be scattered like ashes into the wind of nothingness.

Pride will destroy the smallest thread that could have weaved and mended the broadest love covering into the most beautiful quilted tapestry that covers them for a lifetime.

Chapter One

It is unconditional love that will serve as the cement to pave the road toward successful reconciliation in the relationship. And will soar you like eagles on a carpet ride into marital bliss until death do you part.

Unconditional love will thrust you forward and never backwards. This love never destroys another soul but builds them up. This method of love will find comfort where there was none. It will build faith in the relationship and give hope against hope. It will bathe in abnegation and envelope itself in sacrifice and giving.

Unconditional love will soothe, comfort and put at ease all aggravation; it will provide peace in the worse storm. It will conquer hurt, pain and replace them with fresh oil of healing, peace and joy. It has the capacity to take nothing and make something. It will absorb hate and pour out fountains of love. This kind of love is a wonderful thang.

Two

Bone Dry On the Outside, Wet On the Inside

In defense of women who is a tower of strength which enables her to go through life vicissitudes and still maintain her status quo, her gravitas, pulchritudinous splendor, and it is amazing how she can sometimes suffer from PMDD (Premenstrual Dysphoric Disorder) which causes severe changes in their bodies around the time of her flowering and never diminish her femininity.

The most remarkable characteristic about her is she is the only human being that births life into this world.

These vast changes in her body is known to get in the way of small chores in day to day living and at times she does not feel like being around people, sometimes she doesn't feel so aesthetically pleasing to those who love her the most, especially you mister.

During those times, she can hardly concentrate on school or work and there are moments she becomes so irritated her desires is to be left alone.

It is significant during this period in her life that she is not miss-understood but pampered with unconditional love. It's not the time for scolding but holding, and molding. It becomes difficult for her to explain her mood swings when some of her senses are unbalanced.

A woman cannot explain what she does not understand, and what's understood don't need any explaining. Be patient with her and give her space during these few emotional days in her life.

The man in her life can either make or break the beauty of springtime in the relationship and lead it into darkness of a long cold winter of frozen passions by misdirecting emotions that are already out of control.

Man, must not be insensitive during these sensitive times in her life and calm them with patience for the time necessary; until she's relaxed with herself and desires pleasure again.

Most importantly patiently love her unconditionally which sooths mixed emotions and builds her up during her down times.

Any woman who feels the benignity of another when she is troubled will appreciate the consideration applied. The man must patiently nurture mixed emotions until she is emotionally stable again. Then she is apt to bring more pleasure of the same she has applied in the past; and she is so very capable of applying more in the future.

Caring and understanding her at her low point will become most rewarding when she reaches her high point, she will bring it like never before.

Don't allow a once a month chemically imbalanced emotion to cause her to become motionless in your bedroom the rest of the month.

You can bet your bottom dollar if she became cold toward you, it is very likely at some point she will become warm toward someone else who appears to understand her during troubled times.

According to research there are reasons for this high rate of covenant breakups and miss trust; it is because someone else is giving her moral support and simple things like attention and conversation that the husband is not applying to her life at the dinner table or in the bedroom, or because the woman's low self-esteem is lifted-up by someone outside of the marriage.

It must be considered that today's woman has more financial power due to education, promotions in the workforce that enables her ability of exposure to the varieties and spices of life.

Consequently, the woman can afford to find a sense of trust elsewhere if self-esteem to build her up is not applied at home.

Chapter Two

Don't Take Her for Granted!

Don't allow another to appreciate the gift intimately that God gave to you. Let nobody become more complimentary pertaining to her over all character and beauty than you do. Complement her fragrance, the way she wears her hair, the color of her nails, and her pedicured feet every time you meet her. There is something inside of a woman that turns her on, fires her up when she is admired by the man in her life.

Why do you think they spend countless hours in the beauty shop and run home to you smiling, is it just to be ignored? WAKE UP MAN!!

Wake up foolish man and consider how much time she spends in the beauty shop preparing herself for attention, and she is going to get it.

In fact, at some time or another everybody need a pat on the back. When a woman doesn't get her pat on the back at home she will find a way to get a pat on the butt elsewhere. And she has the appeal, financial power to go and get it anywhere she pleases. The remedy for whatever her issues are and all her idiosyncratic behaviors is unconditional love. If the man doesn't apply it he takes the chance of losing the only conscious being that's suitable and valuable to him.

The lack of unconditional love will leave one sitting in a sea of ambiguity and enigmas searching for the synthesis to heal brokenness and hoping for a life raft that will float them in harmony to the shores of emotional, sexual and sensual safety. Don't take that chance!

Oftentimes this can lead to low self-esteem bitterness and distractions, which can result in a man using uncontrolled energy going where he doesn't need to be. And end up feeling bad about his-self because he gave so much of himself to where he shouldn't be at the cost of where he should be.

The nude club is what it is, a NUDE CLUB, but there is someone at home in your bed nude and burning with desire.

Chapter Two

Instead of applying his energy to the original attraction, he gives way to the foreign distraction.

Some men self-destruct when the void of love and companionship avoids him. Many men try and find solace in nightclubs, drinking and chasing strange women.

Why look for a bush in the forest when you have a rose at home. "He who picks a rose must accept the thorn it bears," a rose does not lose its fragrance just because it has a thorn, yes, she made a mistake, yes her once a month issue caused her to become easily irritated, but what about your bad breath after drinking in the club, what about your bad smelling feet after the workout in the gym?

Some men experimentation with drugs and alcohol trying to escape the coldness of a winter's heart, has allowed him to acquiesce to another instead of drawing her home, now realizes she was the epitome of springtime and summer in his life. Some men lose themselves in loneliness and despair walking around in darkness because he allowed the light of their love life to burn out.

If you began the flame you can blaze a fire.

Once the man patiently and painstakingly observes the body language of his mate and lights a fire that ignites every passionate emotion in the woman by the application of unconditional love; it penetrates her heart and mind, and into every fiber of her being.

Even the hair in hairy places on her body will be sensitive to your touch.

You can be thousands of miles away from her and your voice will create a sensual mood, she will get out of bed and put on your favorite thongs; pull them off again or pull them to the side so that you can talk to her and excite her into many sexual climaxes, it's called phone sex.

Her imagination is completely uninhibited and relaxed by unconditional love. When a woman feels your love for her she will literally reach the apex of sexual satisfaction by following your instructions on the phone. You can talk to her and she is lubricated automatically. Unconditional love is a powerful wonderful thing.

*Call me until you come back home!
What a beautiful time we have together
when you call me on the cell phone.*

Friendship after an Intimate Relationship

Is it better to bring closure to an intimate relationship and remain friends or should we avoid closure and remain enemies?

It is the opinion of the writer that there is never closure remaining enemies with someone you've been intimate with.

You are mendacious to think that you can become sexually and emotionally involved with someone and have complete closure, because emotionally that person has a passionate place or emotional scar inside of your heart; a feeling or emotion that you will ultimately carry over into another relationship that does not deserve the baggage you are bringing.

The new relationship is starving for a new beginning with a clean slate. This person took you at face value; but here you come with garbage held inside from the past.

If there is garbage in; it must come out at some time or another. When mess is compound on top of mess you create a bigger mess.

You may empty trash out of your home once a week, but trash must be emptied out of your relationship daily.

Do not fool yourself; it's very difficult to part from someone that you've had an ultimate love affair with and experienced life together.

It becomes very easy to part from those you've only had a good time with or enjoyed in passing, but when someone has hung in there with you through thick and thin, for better or for worse, it is almost impossible to lose all sociable ties with that lover. But to avoid the potential foolishness that sometimes causes violent behavior, muster up as much unconditional love as possible.

You can abrogate the course of dislike or hate and allow patience and understanding to move you into friendship.

Try to establish a wonderful relationship with the person that may have broken bad when loneliness and thoughts of how they gave you a part of their life or the best years of their lives set in.

Later in life you may need that person who you know cared for you, for whom you are and they may come to your rescue in old age when you need them the most.

Never step on her toes that are connected to her ass you may have to kiss later. Don't burn a bridge you may have to cross again!

We cut down a lot of things we just ought to keep and keep a lot of things we ought to cut down.

I know of a situation where an ex-lover, went about her life with someone else and the gentleman remained her friend, supported and respected her in friendship. Consequently, the woman has come to his aid numerous of times and employs and helps him with his son.

Don't carry hate or dislike for anyone to your grave; when unconditional love can leave a lasting friendship of life and peace.

Unconditional love will make friends with someone, even though you may have lost them as your lover.

There are a few things that's essential for a wholesome relationship with a woman, the first is lots of love, plenty of attention, and some sense of security; then we can add on some patience and kindness coupled with allowing her some space and time to pamper herself.

Allow her the time and give her the money to go and have ear conning. This is a method done by a myomassologist cleaning her ears from accumulated wax. Show her you are concerned about little things concerning her health and beauty.

Also, a myomassologist will perform healing touch massages using a method called rain drops, placing healing oils on her spine to make her feel better. Or suggest that she get what is called a bio cleansing where she places her feet in sea salt water and it pulls the toxins out of her body through her feet.

Chapter Two

Learn to pamper your woman in area's that will keep her healthy and happy. Let the mind body and soul come together freely to release the pent-up emotions of stress and anxiety from her occupational hazardous day.

Fill her tub with bubbles and essential oils. Let the flicker of many scented lighted candles warm her body, share sweet words of love to relax her mind, inviting her desires and energy to collide into a ravenous urge for exciting foreplay and love making.

Exercise with her, show total interest in her becoming healthier. Shower together, cut off cell phones; in fact leave them out of the bed room, instead of a burning radiation from the cell phone, burn candles of Jasmine and Lavender.

Submerging her emotions in loves until you emerge and converge gently inside her with a drop the bomb energy that explodes and burst together, seemingly as numerous as the stars in the sky that brightens every sexual fiber of her being. Then stick your chest out and declare, "How do you like me now."

Expressing love to a woman is different than what most men think it is.

A woman feels loved when she is held and kissed daily, and finds a card on her pillow when she comes home. Love to a woman is a walk in the park holding hands together.

She Love to hold hands walking along the beach, sitting in the park, going for an afternoon ride. Love her; trust her to go shopping after giving her money to shop with.

The average man spends much more on his car or golf game than it would take to send a woman to the mall to buy some sexy panties to please him with. #boomboomboom.

The car or golf clubs cannot cook one meal or clean him up if he becomes ill.

And if you think you can put your penis in a golf bag or the gas tank to reach sexual satisfaction; then you are ill beyond sexual healing.

Chapter Two

I'M WOMAN WHO NEEDS SEXUAL HEALING

Why not keep her satisfied who can satisfy you?

I dare you to be alone with me and ask me to dance naked with you or for you. If you want to witness true felicity with me put on some music while we're alone and dance with me; please allow me to express myself with any parts of my body anyway I feel at that moment.

Make a joyful noise when she sexually invites you into her body (holler like a wild man, be ravished with her love) and watch her respond with more explicit expressions. Don't judge her; enjoy her with unconditional love.

Don't frequent a club looking for a strange, wild sexual woman when you have the strangest wildest sexiest woman already with you. It's what you make or mold it to be.

"Man is a being of power, intelligence, love, and the lord of his own thoughts and castle, man holds the key

to every situation, and contains within himself that transforming agency to will things into reality."
James Allen

"She is lying there waiting for you to request her to do something freaky to you. The woman desires to do some different stuff. This is a man's world, but it would be nothing without a woman or a girl."
James Brown

A man can monitor a situation and bring the best out of it. Bring out those dormant feelings that have been waiting to be released in her from the first time she laid eyes on you. All she wants to know is when she finishes her wild things; will you still love her unconditionally tomorrow?

We must also understand that oral sex and such terms, as tea bagging in sexual intercourse is more prevalent in the bedroom today.

Conventional intercourse will always be good; however, the sexual revolution has caused so many other positions and places other than the bedroom for sexual desires and enhancement. Some enhancements could hinder the relationship if the sexual partner is not ready for spontaneous changes.

There are not many intimate moral standards in a traditional sexual affair, they just don't exist anymore. It becomes critical to drink from your own fountain and keep your relationship as healthy as possible.

Sex in the world today has taken on another meaning. It may be difficult to hold on to a relationship by just doing it. Those days are almost gone; you must put some hot conversation, dip in your hip and some glide in your stride and some sho-nuff in your stuff these days.

Most salads come with more than lettuce and tomatoes, that's old stuff. You got to mix it up with croutons, cucumbers, onions and garlic, the right salad dressing and other stuff in the bowl these days if you want a variety which is the spice of life.

I don't care if you are the president, the Pope or the preacher, if you don't spend quality time with a woman she will find someone who will.

Your money can be as long as the Declaration of Independence, your pockets can be as deep as the Grand Canyon, but if you're not playing with it talking dirty to it, turning it around and upside down, you are mendacious to yourself to think you have a hold on the woman.

GOOD GIRLS GONE WILD

Have you dated the girl with the quiet personality, with wire-rimmed glasses, or very pretty girl who you thought were stuck up, but when the lights went out she was the (livewire in the room) biggest freak you ever had? Ha! Ha! She fooled you with the best sexual healing.

Women today have more money, more power to expose themselves and explore more things pertaining to their sexual preferences. In some instances the moral fabric of the female gender has broken down in deprived and upper-class areas of society allowing the young girls to experience pleasures of sexual satisfaction beyond her own normal moral values (*In many cases with other women*).

Chapter Two

It is the opinion of the writer that the weaker of the two women the fem is searching for something that men did not apply in their lives. Young girls mature faster than young men who has not matured enough to give her what she desires from a man.

The stronger one called the butch seems to offer understanding where the fem was miss-understood by the boy. If she is miss-understood, she has this proclivity to think someone else will tolerate or take the time with her to understand her.

So, she run into the arms of someone that pretends to identify with her pain or mixed up emotions, who pretends to know what she is going through. Who better knows another woman's body or pain than another woman who's been hurt by the same male gender?

Even the butch girl has been hurt, sometimes molested by someone that misunderstood her. So, she dawns Timberlines or sneaker's, turns her ball cap backwards, but she cannot turn the truth into a lie, every time she takes a shower and look in the mirror the truth of nature is there, she is woman.

What could abrogate this foolishness and waste of time in both women lives is the application of unconditional love by a man.

We have an up-coming generation whose very skimpy attire, tattoos and piercing in private places suggest that anything goes. And sex is not only the main course of the menu, but dessert too.

Why would very attractive young ladies with the most perfect figure have the patience to endure the pain of having a tattoo placed at the lower part of her back; just above her butt, then squeeze into hip hugger jeans dawn the sexiest top; bend over so that you can see it all; if she was not trying to be sexually attractive. Let us not fool ourselves, our young people are having sex, and most of it is wild and kinkier than we can imagine.

Recent stats have proven that one out of seven high school girls are pregnant. I don't believe in the stork, I do believe that our young people are having sex more than we think. All of them have cell phones to communicate and connect sexually when we are fast asleep.

Most of the programs and music today are sexually explicit. Our youth have the same human bodies, passions, feelings as we when we were young, they are more youthful and dynamic today than we could have ever imagined; they are more exposed and more uninhibited than we were.

Let's face a fact; humans are going to have sex. I'm not here to defend the right or the wrong in your home pertaining to your children. They know it's wrong, why do you think they hide and do it?

We know it's wrong because we don't desire to bear the possible brunt from the results of sexual promiscuity at such an early age. But whatever the outcome; it will take unconditional love to heal any vestiges left from it and bring closure to it.

There is a sexual revolution today that would make the revolution of the sixties and the days of Woodstock, seem like Sunday school. There is nothing new, except the girls are not Hippies like it was in the sixties but from middle to upper class society who don't mind showing off big tits and bear butts on national television.

They don't mind French kissing and bumping clits to express their sexual pleasure pretending that there is more to life than having a man. After their experience with lesbian illusion, most will come to the realization that it is more than lesbian life, and the more is to have a real man that loves them unconditionally.

However, after all the bumping and grinding, licking and lapping, drinking and sinking into a sea of false fantasy the question should come into play, *"Where is the beef bone?" After the booty, luscious, the games and the toys; where are the boys?*

Man, can take great pride that certain voids in a woman's life are only fulfilled by man.

Two female plugs can never bring enough juice to procreate. Man, can take pride that foreplay between two women is not the real game. It takes a heavy hitter with a bat to knock the ball out of the park. It takes a champion to knock the component out; and only the man possess that kind of training and equipment.

So, brothers just wait with unconditional love until all the faking and shaking is over and just hold your *PIECE*, she will return.

Negative Turns Positive

From this sexual revolution of very gorgeous, educated, promiscuous and sexually confused young ladies will emerge an amalgamation into society many beautiful potential house wives and mothers.

They will emerge from the depths of self-grandiose into some of the most trusted companions and friends a man can possess. Because they will have tried everything sexually possible only to find that they needed a man in the first place.

Let's face a fact; and that is everybody has been with somebody in sexuality and became aware of the fact I don't belong here, even you. Chances are most men will never know of the woman's past abstruse relationships. Whatever her behaviors were past and present it is unconditional love that conquerors all.

Some men have tried to be conversant with other men, other things, masturbated while viewing strange snuff stuff in strange places. Because once again man mind is likening to a garden, when the Gardner don't weed out the garden, the weeds overtake the fruit, so today pull the impure thoughts out of your mind and you will stop accusing the woman of strange behaviors because of your strange behaviors in the past.

"The farthest distance in the world is yesterday."

As women mature genetically mentally, it is far more evident that the vicissitudes of life have caused insecurity and that life changes have

Chapter Two

caused the scales of balance to tip toward some improprieties in her life.

Sometimes casual dating turns catastrophic and the woman becomes fearful of relationships. Oftentimes the fear of failure overpowers the need to succeed, (*Nietzsche says*), "*those who have a 'why' can bear with almost any how.*"

Usually a positive is derived from this scenario because now she has quality time to apply herself productively furthering her education or her careers to counter her fears and insecurity's which was caused in past relationships.

She may party and travel extensively which is also educational, while searching for the void that sooths her very nature, which is to love and to be loved.

*The mental capacity of a woman need **COMFORT**, her brokenness needs **MENDING**, her intellect needs **FEEDING**, her ego need **STROKING**, and her vanity need **BALANCING**, her body need a **CARESSER**, her lips need **KISSING**, her breast need **ENJOYING**, her nails* *and feet need PAINTING, her pocket need MONEY, her life need SECURING.*

All her needs can be complimented and appreciated through man's unconditional love, WHEN A MAN LOVE A WOMAN.

GROW UP SO YOU CAN CATCH UP!

Men should prepare for the plethora of gorgeous ladies who will revolve and flood the dating market after experiencing the false sexual fantasies and frivolities of lesbianism.

Their experiences in this realm of sexual fantasies will leave them without child birth and the companionship only found in the male gender. Sisters bumping pearls cannot produce babies, she has secretly longed to birth. Also, the pole she learned to dance on and the sex toy cannot take the place of a man's Johnson. Her desire to tea bag (kiss balls) cannot be duplicated with a toy.

Chapter Two

I would be remiss not to voice the pleasant alarm that out of this awakening of rivers of stored up sexual passion will produce a plethora of nymphomaniacs; not a bad thing except every city will become over populated.

The sexual revolution in the future will become out of control /off the chain. But the man who can get out of self and take full control with unconditional love will have the sexual time of his life with an over populated society of over sexed woman.

I hope that the men of this new generation from Hip Hop through Millennials will mature from their prison mentality and pull up their pants, wash their behinds and become accustomed to an impeccable degree of grooming themselves so that the ladies can become very proud of the gent she's looking up to when the flood gates of these pretty beef consuming girls open to unconditional love.

A mature beautiful educated woman is not looking for a brokaz, dirtyaz, dope smokingaz, jailbirdaz, wife beatingaz, but she is looking for her Boaz. (The book of Ruth).

And stop driving on the freeways like a fool killing yourselves. Please go to school, find a job, start your own business and move out of your mother's house to self-worth and responsibility.

Put the forty down and pick up a pencil, look beyond what's in your pants into the future and see that your purpose in life may not be all rap but to tap into more education to better the world's situation. Some people say money is not everything, *but the last I checked it was up there with oxygen.*

> *"To have what others don't have, you must be willing to do what others won't do."*

Since many women have been hurt and become frighten of some men, makes it difficult to become conversant with men. And in many cases, she is more prosperous than some men, but possess the capacity to submit to a good man.

Chapter Two

"Only boys are in awe of the woman who is more prosperous than he, a man is over joyed by her accomplishments."

This unique virtue that the independent woman possess gives man the opportunity to partner with her to enhance and harness more prosperity as both are willing to yoke together to bring suitability to their lives so when challenges come they are unshaken, unbreakable in their compatibility and unconditional love.

Unconditional love does not change because of women financial status. It is not intimidated by a woman's lofty position in society, nor is it agitated because of past faults or failures. In fact, it learns to love and support all capriciousness with pity and kindness.

It does not convict but converts. It painstakingly comfort fears, opens locked doors in the woman's heart, secures her life from faults and builds her up from past failures. It says to the worse situation, I love you anyway baby, I love you just the way you are.

It Was There All The Time!

I was flying on Southwest from a speaking engagement and I opened my big mouth about unconditional love with a couple of passengers and the question was asked, is this kind of love attainable?

Is it reality to possess this kind of love without becoming very spiritual? I propose to you that this kind of love was there all the time.

Where the spiritual becomes critical in the relationship, human frailty is subject to weakness even consternation due to life challenges. As Patience runs thin, understanding is limited and weights of life gets heavy. It is during these times we need to look outside of ourselves for strength.

Your wife, your lover, your mate, your significant other whatever you desire to call it had the same faults and fears before you met them as they do now. If you could love them then why not now? Someone said, "what you don't know can't hurt you, I say what you do know can

Chapter Two

heal every one of you." It is transparency, that will make both of you free.

Just because you married her and moved her to a different location does not change her character. If she pulled off her underwear at her mother's house and threw them in the corner for days she will do the same thing at the new address.

In fact, it was at her mother's house where you first pulled her panties to the side and played with her. She is still the same woman and oftentimes she already had a child and a stork did not drop the baby off on her door steps, she lay down with a man and he inserted his penis in her and they reached a climax and she became pregnant; get over it, that experience in her past life does not diminish her gifts, faithfulness or abilities to make you a happy man.

The farthest distance on earth is yesterday!

She left the toothpaste open at her mothers or in her apartment before you moved her in with you. She caught colds in winter and has sinus in the spring, don't you remember stopping by the drug counter for her? She had monthly periods; don't you remember the string? Her breath was not pleasant every morning before you married her.

Have her teeth cleaned or buy a stronger mouthwash, but don't dirty up her mouth by resenting her or washing out the love in her heart for you by hurting her.

It is what it is and your negative attitude won't change it, but unconditional love will endure all when a man loves a woman. He tolerates and often celebrate her faults, failures and fears that were there all the time. Her maybe should not change her from being your baby.

She has made plenty of mistakes in life and will make more. She was a Mall shopper all the time. If you go to the Mall today you will see her twenty years ago by herself or with her best girlfriend dressed in tight jeans walking in and out of every store.

Chapter Two

The young girls you see in the Mall today was your girl twenty years ago laughing and giggling, and flirting with the cell phone and sometimes just shopping and not buying anything. The only difference their pants were not so tight and their navel was not showing.

But you were attracted to her just as she was. You did not hold a confirmation hearing, or march her to the judgment hall for screening.

You accepted her with all her faults fears and failures. Now that you have discovered them and must live with them, as she must live with yours and you do have plenty of them and often more than she; do all that you can to love her anyway.

So, she is on her period, well you have bad breath, well somedays she has an attitude, you have smelly feet, wake up, suck it up, get up, man up, fix her up, stop whining, take her to the movies or to dinner and live it up.

Three

Obsession or Depression

Most humans feel sad at one time or another. A passing bad mood is not considered clinical depression. Many things can contribute to a bad mood such as the lack of finances, impatience for the other person, miss-understandings, poor communication, overwhelming monthly expenses.

Real depression is one of the most common psychological disorders and can go unrecognized for years because of the compounding of many different symptoms.

Symptoms of depression can include a consistently depressed mood; the woman can become irritable, loss of interest or pleasure in all or nearly all activities, sleeplessness, or a desire to sleep all the time. She can acquire persistent feelings of guilt or worthlessness, fatigue, difficulty concentrating. She may complain of headaches and backaches and even suicidal thoughts.

If someone accidentally dropped a baby and the baby became crippled from the fall, it is not the baby's fault for the deformity. The woman is not at fault for clinical depression. The primary cause is a shortage in the brain of a chemical called serotonin.

Serotonin acts as a neurotransmitter, or substance that carries impulses from one nerve cell to another.

It is the opinion of the writer that we never downplay herbal healing and modern psychiatry which states that depression is a physical condition that expresses itself in emotional symptoms.

However, there is a virtue called unconditional love that covers all areas of depression. You can love a person out of the gloom of wanting to commit suicide, to the light of; I shall live and not die.

If the doctor can't find a pill to help and the psychiatrist need help themselves; the infinite creator has given us a medicine that will cure any state of depression; it will take unconditional love to pull her through.

It does not help today's woman that many men are in prison, some have become gay, and others are on drugs and the ultimate foolishness men having sex on the down low.

If the woman of today has become more powerful, promiscuous, liberal, lustful and in most cases, exposed to more sexual experiences, then the man of today must counter this movement to favor him with something of substance. It is not about catching up; it is about catching on.

The only hope in slowing down this locomotive is what she has desired from childhood; unconditional love. Get on board mister or get left.

"Get in or get to steppin." Martin Lawrence

When it becomes impossible for man to settle sexual issues with woman, then it is time to look toward a greater source. Dare not allow false power, promiscuity or any other virtue to work against your home when you can nurture and build it with unconditional love.

When a man loves a woman, he will give of himself and make sacrifices when necessary for the woman. He will always look past her faults and see her needs.

Unconditional love is extravagant love that surpasses the boundaries of selfishness, criticisms, shortcomings and idiosyncratic behaviors.

One man's junk becomes another man's treasure because of unconditional love.

Unconditional love is unlimited and surpasses all knowledge. The infinite master of the universe created all of us and we all possess the capacity to love. That's why there is somebody for everyone.

Chapter Three

Ask yourself what is the bond or social glue that hold two people together for life who are very poor, very old but will stay together until death part them?

The people who you will pass up deeming them to be too bad or too ugly or too crippled; is a lover and companion for someone else, your ugly duckling is a beauty queen to another man. Your elephant man is a Romeo or Joe Millionaire to another woman.

If the story of John Merrick (*the elephant man*), is true and I have every reason to believe it is; then it was unconditional love that inspired him to a sense of self-worth and heighten his self-esteem where he had none.

This man was so disfigured that he wore a sack over his head because of his horrific visage. And if my recollection serves me right it was a wealthy woman who loved him unconditionally, enough to shower him with gifts and embraced him with love and respect.

The worst looking person in the world can have a virtue from God that flows from the inside of them that's loveable. On the other hand, the most beautiful person in the world can have a character flaw in him or her that's detestable.

There are some people who are not attractive on the outside, but as soon as they open their mouth you can feel the love that permeates from the inside.

On the other hand, you have people who are drop-dead gorgeous on the outside but as soon as they open their mouth you wonder why a person with all those good looks could talk so vulgar, and at the same time be such an airhead.

Wealth on the inside has nothing to do with wealth on the outside; a beautiful person is a beautiful person whether they have money, good looks or not. (*Beauty is only skin deep but ugly is to the bone*).

It is a true saying "Out of the abundance of the heart the mouth speaks," and "beauty is only skin deep."

Much of the outside is not connected to the inside and much of the inside is not connected to the outside.

Chapter Three

I can give a woman more money and she can be just as ignorant as if she were broke. I can buy her a bigger car and if she was a drunk in the small car she will become a bigger car drunk driver. So much is not connected.

Some of the most attractive people have the lowest self-esteem and a plethora of issues. Most people that appear not to have problems have the most. It will take unconditional love to hang with the look that fooled you by its cover.

We cannot judge a look by its cover, but whatever the cover is there is someone that will take it. It is diversity in the world that keeps life exciting and enriches all our lives.

You may say well, it's just lust. However, I differ with you, because people usually lust after those who are very attractive. Men usually lust over the woman with the shapely legs; full breast and buttocks that's clad in something skimpy.

But what about the man who is holding tightly to the woman who is not voluptuous with full breast, big hips, and may possess skinny legs, dress homely? Joe Tex picked it up in a song years ago, *"give me the woman with the skinny legs." Everything is not for everybody.*

It is the writer's opinion that we are all innately born with a measure of unconditional love. We were all made in the likeness of our creator who is love; and even after the fall of man in the garden when Adam first sinned against God we did not completely lose our ability to love one another.

It would not have been commanded by God that we love our neighbor as ourselves, if we did not have the capacity and ability to fulfill this serious issue. (Give me a kiss I am your neighbor…Out Kast).

Something inside of me must see something inside of you that others deem as ugly or beauty and its unconditional love.

It is key and critical to understand it's unconditional love that transcends all boundaries of sins ugliness to lift us up when we are down, free us when we are bound by some of the very negative vestiges and scars that were often forced upon us because of life itself.

> *"Forgiveness is the fragrance in the vile that is shed on the heel that crushed it."*

Unconditional love will transcend the ugliness of the deposits placed in our lives by wrong relationships or dysfunctional families we've encountered. The same love can save any relationship that will inevitably encounter antitheses between lovers resulting from faults and failures (Conflict is healthy if it brings about resolve).

MYSTERY UNFOLDED

This is a great mystery; the union between the husband and wife; man, and woman, however it intimates the relationship between God and the church; "the good book says," He gave the ultimate sacrifice for her when he allowed himself to die that she may live. The good book also speaks of His son and the resurrection guaranteeing life eternal for his bride; which is the church. And of course, the church has its faults and failures.

But the Lord is her protector, guide and keeper (Ps.23).

When a man loves a woman, he will always rise to the occasion to make life more comfortable for her. The woman's guarantee that the man truly love her is the portions of himself he will sacrifice to protect and keep her.

Will the man willingly give up some things he love to make her happy, will he give up the football game for a family outing? The woman's faithfulness, grace and charm has much to do with getting anything she desires from man.

Many women down through the ages have not proven themselves worthy of this sacrificial covenant; and have broken it with unfaithfulness.

However unconditional love will empower the man to love her back into his embrace; accepts her as she is, love and forgive her for her weaknesses.

Chapter Three

When a man loves a woman; wife beating, child neglect and all types of physical or mental abuse is vicariously replaced with love; and it will become very difficult for man with a renewed mind and awareness of the power of unconditional love to cheat on the woman who he cares for.

When a man loves a woman the very thought of bringing home a disease to the lady who satisfies his sexual, social and spiritual appetite is appalling to his nature. Man's respect for his woman will not allow his conscious to think of defiling the area where real love and love making is to take place.

I remember my younger years in the south when our parents would preserve jams and jellies at a certain time of the year. The preservation of the jams and jellies consist of cooking the fruit, placing it in a clean jar, sealing it with a rubber seal and capping it real tight. Consequently, the jam would remain sweetly preserved for years.

Man can preserve his relationship with woman; simply keep the heat going; just tighten things up and seal it with unconditionally love. "Preserves are sweet after the heat, and things can get tight after the fight. "Break up is to make up." The second time around is sometimes better than the first time.

It is in the making up where the lover applies unconditional love. What's in the past is behind you, let it remain where it is; in the past. Let by gone be by gone and don't bring up anything she has done but look at what she can be to you in the future.

A real man and lover will not only look at the woman for who she is; but for who she can become. Her value should not be predicated on what was; but on what she has gone through and overcame.

Don't push her away, experiences have made her more valuable than you think.

The farthest distance in the world is yesterday!

No man desires that the woman he loves is lured into the arms of another. What kind of man

Chapter Three

is it that desires the personal and private parts of the woman's body that satisfy him is shared with another man?

No! This is not a pleasant feeling at all. But how many affairs have you had and she continued to love and make love to you as if you were the last man on earth. What is good for the goose is good for the gander.

Yes! She became weak and made a mistake, but she is not a mistake, she is a human being with faults, and the creator made her the weaker vessel.

From the beginning, she was tricked and confused with what to do for you and with you.

What have you done lately to strengthen her?

Many separations divorces and even death in relationships has occurred when a mate is caught in the act of loving and love making with another outside of the home.

When this covenant is violated it could bring about tragedy. Somebody please just tighten things up! It takes strength to tighten up, especially if you are the one who has lightened up. The woman reflects her man. You will know a tree by the fruit it bears

WOMEN LOVE POWER AND PURPOSE!

It is critical for us to understand that God will allow problems in all our lives just to disseminate his power to fulfill his purpose,

Our beloved mother Eve was given power in the womb and purpose to begin the progeny of mankind after the forming of man and the beginning of creation. She is the mother of all living (Gen. 3:20).

We basically know her for the mistake she made in the garden by allowing Satan to deceive her, eating of the tree of the knowledge of good and evil which was sin against God.

Chapter Three

She gave forbidden fruit to her husband Adam; thus, causing sin and death to all of creation. As a result, she had to get through the curse imposed on her by the creator which was the sentence to travail in child bearing to receive the power to become the mother of all living. She had to go through something to get to purpose.

> *"Hardship prepares an ordinary person for an extraordinary destiny."* C. S. Lewis

Though in one area she may become weak, but look at her resilience, how she brings mankind into the world from between urine and feces.

Today is Feb. 8th, the winter season is here in West Bloomfield Mi.; my daughter Kim is three thousand miles away in L. A. Calif.; She has brought forth my first grandson Eli and granddaughter Isley Anne my second grand baby.

As I sat in my easy chair a few ticks ago and thought of my darling child, I also thought of you who may be with child, or can't bear children now.

I pondered over how I can find some research to be very definitive in encouraging you on such a very sensitive matter. And without the proclivity to entice you into religion. I'm sensitive enough to know that there is a book that all other books seem to glean from in one way or another.

I'm also an old movie buff, love TCM movies and I listen to the lines spoken very carefully by the actors, and from love stories to Dracula, Wolfman to Dr. Jekyll and Hyde, and what more can we say about Cecil B. Demille and The Ten Commandments.

If you will carefully listen to dialogue, just about 99% of movies new and old will quote something whether subliminal or direct from the bible.

Hollywood have always encouraged us from the bible to make their stories appear true to us, and they have done a pretty good job, because we the people have made them very rich by going to the movies that make us laugh, cry and sometimes pattern ourselves after some of the characters.

Chapter Three

Today I cannot help but think of your purpose in the world in a greater sense, in the fact that God placed the power of child birth in your womb for bringing forth life into the world.

There is a lady in the bible named Sarah whose name means princess, she was the wife of Abraham the father of faith: she became so insecure, and feeling powerless without purpose because her womb was barren she gave her hand maiden Hagar to her husband Abraham to bear a child in her stead.

This was not approved by the creator, this was done by choice, notwithstanding, God blessed the situation but her child Ishmael was not the child who was called to fulfill his ultimate plan, nevertheless the child had purpose.

So, the moral of this case scenario is whether one decide to adopt or use artificial insemination, the Creator will bless the effort and is able to fulfill His purpose in any given situation.

The creator can take an abandon child, orphan, and the physically challenged and make something purposeful and beautiful where others thought ugliness and nothing.

It was important for women during those times to bear a man child to carry on the family legacy and inherit the family wealth. You are not alone and certainly not a mistake or not favored by God because you cannot bear children now in your life. But thanks, be to God who gives you the victory to love yourself until your tomorrow becomes better than your yesterday.

He gave Sarah strength to become pregnant at ninety years old, so it appears to me that with God all things are possible. Sarah received seed while past age because she found him faithful who had promised. Her purpose was fulfilled to deliver the seed Isaac through which all the nations of the earth is blessed.

The child you are waiting to birth has a greater purpose in life than you could ever ask or think, so it is worth the wait. Just maybe the time is not Gods time and the man in your present life is not ready or royal enough for you and the royal baby.

Chapter Three

It is my desire to give many women hope against hope by sharing this discourse of bible truths with you. God gave a harlot (whore) power and purpose. A prostitute has the power of persuasion. So, God used her reputation to draw two military men into her house for helping Gods people to reach the Promised Land.

God's real purpose was two-fold in the life of Rahab the harlot; and that was to use her to help his people into the Promised Land and to save her and her family. I hope you are encouraged by Rehabs story in the book of Joshua.

If she found favor in the eyes of God, you can find favor too. Favor with God can give you power and purpose which is worth more than money. Favor will get you all the money you need and purpose in God will enable you to help save a soul which is worth more than money.

It is a tremendous and interesting observation in reading the story of Deborah in the book of Judges the fourth chapter which depicts power and purpose. She used her power of prophecy to persuade Barak to fight and become victorious over a multitude of men.

She did not usurp her authority to fight as a man, but to encourage the man to fight and his purpose was to win as a man. What is your purpose for your man? Is your purpose to belittle him or to help empower him?

What can we say about Hanna, who did not give up because her womb was shut up? She used the power of prayer to cry unto God until her womb was fruitful: baring a son that she offered up to God to live for God.

If your problem is a barren womb and you desire a child, use the power of prayer and purpose in your heart that the child will serve God and maybe he will have mercy on you. Is there anything too hard for Him?

I'm sure there are many women, who have found themselves in an adulteress relationship, became pregnant and decided to abort the child or place it up for adoption.

Chapter Three

It is here where Bathsheba enters the picture as an adulteress woman with King David. Although the affair was done in sin; and the first child died, God is a God of second chances giving her power in her womb to bring forth another son named Solomon who became King and the wisest richest man who ever lived.

My favorite lady of all times is Queen Esther who used her power of beauty to find favor with the king under abnormal circumstances. On the third day, she put on her royal apparel which means she took her time to get dressed for the occasion. Then she stood in the inner court of the Kings house and maintained her poise as a lady.

The King sat upon his royal throne in the royal house and when he saw Esther the queen standing in the court as she obtained favor in his sight and was offered half of the kingdom.

She used the power of her pulchritude to entice a king, but her purpose was to save a nation. My question to you is are you using your God given gifts to help others, or is your purpose selfish?

We conclude this short discourse of powerful women with purpose to enlighten all readers of the fact that there have always been women, through child birth or family genes, were gifted with power to fulfill Gods purpose to help mankind.

In our conclusion, we must present the wife of Zacharias Elisabeth the mother of John the Baptist, who was righteous before God, she walked in all the commandments and ordinances of the Lord blameless, but she had no child.

Barren, well stricken in years which intimates she was too old to have children, this was shameful during this period of history.

But God gave her power to bare John the Baptist the forerunner for our Lord Jesus Christ. Her purpose was to bring in the preacher that prepared the way of the Lord.

The story of Elisabeth should encourage older women; you not only have purpose and power in old age but you can also have pleasure.

Chapter Three

Now the things we have spoken concerning women who have power and purpose this is the sum. It is here where we must present Mary the mother of Jesus who was given power by the Holy Ghost. The power of the highest overshadowed her and the Holy thing that was born of Mary is the Son of God. Her purpose was to bring forth the savior of the world.

God gave her the power to watch her son suffer, and die the most crucial death. Her purpose was to see him raised from the dead and be empowered by him to be a witness for him to win many souls alive.

Where is your power to persist when the man in your life is going through difficult times, and what is your purpose in his life?

THE DUTY OF MAN!

Mortal man is innately born with a sense of being a protector, securing his personal family that God gave him; especially his woman. Some men have worked themselves to death to bring home the bacon for the woman.

Have you ever wondered why men of old worked in coal mines, steel mills, chopped cotton, bought and sold goods, became adventurous, fought wars, left their nativity to go out and make good just to have enough money to take care of the woman?

It is mendacious to think you were not innately born to love and care for the woman.

There were times when women were predominately housewives who kept the home clean; the bacon cooked and bare the children; while men bare the heat of the midday sun, the dust of the fields to earn wages for the family's security.

My dad worked the Mulga coal mines in Alabama, was congested with black lung and died from the dust of black coal so that my mother and my siblings would have comfort and security.

Some men have sacrificed their whole lives, leaving the south going north to find work, that the woman's life is secure from cold and hunger.

Chapter Three

Man loves woman; and it is not his desire their covenant is violated while he's earning a living. He expects his helper to keep what God has given him; especially her body and to enhance what he creates. *maintaining his home.*

Eternal life in Paradise was denied because of Adams love and trust for Eve. Kingdoms have been sacrificed because of man's love for women.

God is the first to initiate unconditional love. I read somewhere that He so loved the world he gave his only begotten son. Now anyone who will do that must love the people he gave his son for.

If my condition was in sin before a Holy God which causes disconnection from Him and knowing I'm just down right messed up according to the standards of God who is perfect in all His ways. For him to love us in the condition that we're in He must love us unconditionally.

While God has a voluntary relationship to everything he has a necessary relationship to nothing!

So, it could not have been my ability, my looks or my efforts that caused him to give someone as precious as his only begotten son for me. I had no ability because He offered him up knowing I was messed up.

The sincerity of it all is that God was looking for a lover so desperately that he did not care how we smelled, how debilitated we were in our soul or how demoralizing we were socially and characteristically. As a matter of fact, he was looking for a lover that had been beat down, to help them up to feel good about themselves again. We should always build up the one we profess to love.

You cannot keep some one down unless you remain the same position with them.

He was looking for someone naked so that he could clothe them for better self-esteem. We should assist the one we love who represents us to always look good so that they always feel good about themselves. He was looking for someone who the rest of society had given up on so that he could give them back as a gift to society.

Suppose the woman that you discard as if she is nobody become somebody and get filthy rich when you need a helping hand. The same people you meet going up, you meet them coming down. No matter the outcome of the sexual relationship, always remain friends.

He was looking for a wrong doing lover so that he could make them right. Sometimes the woman doesn't have all the right qualities according to what you desire. But look at the good and the positive; everybody has something good and positive about them.

Anybody who will give their only son for me must see something in me that I don't see. Unconditional love is a many splendor thing.

We are also commanded to enhance the gifts he has given to us. Which is indicative of the relationship between man and woman; both should share their gifts of love to enhance life for each other and mankind.

Mark Anthony was seduced by Cleopatra and I read somewhere that Alexander the Great biggest war was conquering the heart of Josephine. One of the Monarchs of England gave up his crown because of his love for a Canadian lover.

The wisest and richest man who ever-lived, King Solomon turned away from God because of his love for women. His father King David; a man, after Gods own heart killed and committed adultery because of love at first sight.

Modern men today fall on their knees and propose to woman, begging for her hand in marriage; and vow to care for her for a lifetime because of the love and affection that only a woman can give.

Wealthy men who could afford to purchase sex from ten women per day have committed suicide because of one woman's love and affection that evaded him. There are men serving time in prison because of their desire to properly provide for the woman. They sold drugs, robbed, stole and killed to get money to please a woman. Love is a many splendor thing!

Since marriage is the essential thing to do and is ordained by God; let us consider the beginning of marriage and love making according to Gods order.

Marriage a la Carte'

It is significant for us to understand that some people have not found their soul mate because of impatience. When you find that very special someone, it's miraculous.

Marriage is honorable in all and the bed undefiled. The union between man and woman is sacred and is an honor that the two of you met while on planet earth.

For two to meet and become one with the commitment to spend the rest of their lives together is a miracle within itself.

Out of all the people on earth, she picked you to love and to cherish. We should respect her enough to not defile the sacred place where she lay her head. Why bring a spirit of another which possibly can be a murderous or suicidal spirit into your space?

We will expound on this matter in another chapter. Let's have differences in our relationships but never defilement. Keep that area of your lives sacred. The specificity of your marriage should be guarded daily.

If we are not working on saving the marriage we are giving way to losing it.

It is unconditional love that saves the marriage and it is that same kind of love that will save humans. The same love will reconcile two people back together and save their marriage or relationship. When a man loves a woman, it must be unconditional.

The woman is too complex of an individual to love her in any other fashion. How can you put conditions on someone who carry a baby for nine months deliver it between urine and feces, where the male organ of copulation is penetrated?

Chapter Three

She is so fearfully and wonderfully made that she can have a monthly period and don't die; she can shop all day and don't buy, she can sit in a beauty parlor for hours just to attract a man, make love all night, if the man does it right she cares nothing for the hair, but solely cares about satisfying her mate.

Women of old washed clothes, hang them on clothes lines, cooked three meals a day, ironed everything they washed, bathe the children, comb their hair, walk to the store, shop for the month, and made love to the man at night. In some unfortunate relationships, she has the love and strength to live with flexibility enduring abuse from the man.

How can you put conditions on someone this fascinating and so marvelous? How can you not love this wonderful human being, this fantastic person, this chosen vessel who is the giver of life?

How can you not love unconditionally this woman, this lady, this girl who possess the reproductive system to procreate life into the world; has the only muscle that can satisfy on a normal basis the desires of a man; after she has delivered a baby from the same muscle? She possesses the same virtues as your mother, your sister, your aunt, she's your wife, your lover, your companion, your help, and your friend.

Love her unconditionally and she will love you back.

God did not take her from a bone in man's head so that he could totally dominate her; nor did he take her from a bone in his feet for him to walk on her, but from under his heart for him to love her as he loves himself.

If something precious is given to you, so wonderful and sexy and is a part of you, then it's yours to love and cherish just as you love yourself. And since its given; that makes it a gift for you. When a man loves a woman, he loves a gift from his creator.

It is unwise to miss-use or abuse a precious gift. The gift also has love inside of it. The creator can give but he also can take away. He can make

Chapter Three

what one man deem as trash another man's treasure.

"Therefore, shall a man leave his father and his mother, and shall cleave (hold on at all cost) unto his wife: and they shall be one flesh." Genesis 2: 24

Everything was there in creation when the woman was positioned. Obviously, she is to be taken care of. Even in the curse she was not told to till the ground. She is not to boss the man around or argue all day because the day was made and the order was set when she came. And she is not to get stressed out or over worked.

Don't stress her Bless her!

It was not the creator's intention that the woman is overworked and under paid. Male employers need to know that the so-called liberated women is to be used and not miss-used and certainly not abused.

In all relationships, we should be of some use to each other. Most modern-day systems the man works and secure the home, the woman cook and clean house. Man and woman use each other when having sex. The miss use comes into play when the sex is abused.

The wife does not have any power of her body, but the husband: and likewise, also the husband has no power of his own body, but the wife. Both of you should give way to each other in total ecstasy when making love.

Her body is to be used by the man and likewise, but no one should ever miss-use the other. In the act of harmonious sexual intercourse, the woman is using man's body and he is using her body. If one is causing the other unwanted pain intentionally; then it becomes miss-use.

Stress Test

Show me a woman who is not provided cash or credit cards to purchase for herself or household things and I'll show you a frustrated woman. Frustration causes stress, and stress hinders production.

I believe some employers are prosperous only so that they can help feed a mother and her children. This is Gods way of loving her when there is no male provider. And he does it through those who He made prosperous. I believe Bill Gates is one of the richest men in America because he does so much for those who have little.

God is saying to the woman don't think too hard on things that don't concern you.

The woman is made too delicate to live under stress. Stress is the cause of many diseases. God desires that she remain healthy, loving and fair to look up on. She's a carrier of life, love and not diseases. She is stress free when she is involved in things she desires to do. And her first desire should be to her man who provides.

It is essential the man create atmospheres conducive for a stress-free life for the woman. This desire is nurtured and matured when the woman is loved unconditionally.

She is a help meet to the man (*one who is suitable*) for the man. She is also the ambiance for the garden. Show me an employer who employs beautiful women and I'll show you a busy successful employer.

Right or wrong, the playboy guru who just died out-lasted many other enterprises because of the beautiful flowers that grace his garden.

It's cheaper to keep her.

It's not my call to judge the Playboy Guru or any other man at how he makes his living. There is some good in everything and everybody. I'm simply making a point that well-kept women in a well-kept atmosphere will bring well-kept finances. A well-kept woman is an asset to her husband, because she's a reflection of him. Keep her attire tight and she will always make things right.

She is the only flower in the garden who can satisfy the man. Since she is the only being that has a conscious just as the man, then man should do all he can; even make sacrifices to hold on to the woman.

Bone of my bone and flesh of my flesh.

Man should never enter heated arguments or fight against the woman or the woman against man. Because she is taken from him, bone of his bone and flesh of his flesh. Show me a man who will bruise his own flesh or break his own bones and I will show you a man that's a fool.

Show me a man who will allow the only flower in the garden suitable for him to whither and I'll show you an unwise man. A reflection of you should be presentable always.

> *The garden is only as beautiful as the keeper of the garden keeps it.*

Suppose God did not have order set for us and we could look like anything and do everything contrary to Gods order. Well some people do it anyway but they are dead looking derelicts, junkies and misfits. The man who loves his woman will not allow her to appear un-kept; derelict, junkie or misfit.

A man cares nothing for the woman who he allows to look shabby, rough and unpolished. On the other hand, most men will look pass that kind of woman for his personal lover, but in his heart of hearts he will have some compassion for her shabby condition because unconditional love reminds him, his mother is also a woman.

Most men are more compassionate toward a female beggar than a male because of unconditional love received from the womb of his mother.

For argument sake, if there is a woman who has fallen on hard times and is on the corner begging most men would reach out to her because of his compassion for women derived from unconditional love.

Personally, I'd rather see a man standing by the roadside begging any day than to see a woman catching a bus. It hurt me to think that someone's mother; sister or aunt is homeless and begging because of my love and compassion for women.

I WAS MADE TO LOVE HER

"Husbands love your wives even as Christ also loved the church; and gave his life for it; Wives submit yourselves unto your own husbands, as unto the Lord." Ephesians 5: 25

When the woman is loved cherished and protected as Christ does the church then she reciprocates to the proportion of the love she has received.

We loved God because He first loved us. The creator first loves his creation, the creation observes and appreciates the unconditional love given them and then begins to love God in return.

Likewise, the woman deeply appreciates the application of the love, loving kindness towards her and begins to show her love in return. Give a woman unconditional love, love her when she is on and love her when she is off. Give her your undivided attention and remember the little things are important to her, do the little things and big things will follow.

Invite her to your office now and then, sit down pull her into your lap, just hold her in your arms and tell her this is where you make money to take care of her.

Then take her to lunch or have lunch sent into the office. This gives her a sense of security that she is a part of your whole life.

If you don't work in an office explain to her what you do to make a living. Take her down to the work site, take her to lunch or dinner and give her a nice gift.

Reminisce with her during quality time, remind her where you went on the first date and why you give her nice gifts then observe how she responds to you! Then take her to ecstasy all night long.

Things that men take lightly weigh heavy on women.

Chapter Three

Woman was taken from man after man was created in the likeness of God. As soon as the woman was brought to the man he proclaimed that she was bone of his bones and flesh of his flesh. He instantly loved her who was taken from his rib. They both were naked and not ashamed.

She submitted to the love he had for her. He was not ashamed and she wasn't either.

It is not otherwise recorded so it's the writer's belief that she submitted to her husband for nine hundred and thirty years (Gen. 5:5). Why can't today's woman submit for thirty days?

Be encouraged single/married women because he may love you, oftentimes he does not know how to love you.

You are not helping him with the attitude of not submitting to him. Once again, he loves you, but not the atmosphere you create because of sometimes past experiences that failed you.

Most white men have better jobs, resources, more money, let's face it, white privileges allow them provision where there is lack of unconditional love. So, give the brother a chance because though many odds are against him, working together with him; still you can rise.

Some men will experience the passive humble submissive atmosphere of other women of other races who offers unconditional love and love making and he will gravitate to them. So now you are bitter when you could have been better by doing it Gods way instead of your way.

Be advised or leave it, continue to do it your way or a way, but no man will live in an atmosphere unless it is done THE way.

Submit to the man (not a pair of pants, sport coat or a boy, but a man) you have chosen for a life partner. He will secure your life, and buy you nice things, the new home, the new car, the Louis Vuitton's, etc., etc. (it works and caused men to become a constant giver who was always the taker.

Why do you think the nude bars remain full? Because the ladies inside are friendly and already dressed in thongs, Victoria Secret, ready to submit to anything the man can afford.

You don't have to be conversant if you are dating, especially if you are not sure if he is the right one. But you can be loving and kind with unconditional love, use your charm beauty, cross your legs in front of him, give just enough for him to put a ring on it. Don't give up the cow, when a little milk will get it done.

You know you don't desire to sleep alone for the rest of your life. It doesn't hurt to let the man know it is more to you than what meets the eye. When you are married, you can back up the talk by being who you desire to be in the privacy of your atmosphere for loves.

You can be a church girl on Sunday morning, but Tina Turner, Chaka Kahn, a playboy Bunny or a private lap dancer on Sunday night.

Marriage is honorable in all and the bed is undefiled.

You had better wake up and take a lesson from a whore. He is going to bed where she is submissive!

Maybe it will help you to submit to him if you realize it is from him whence you came. And mister, since she came from you it should be nothing enigmatic concerning how to care for her. You know what you like, well she like the same thing.

In other words dude, if you are putting it down right she won't have a problem giving it up right (submitting to you).

If you will notice in the scripture God told the husband to love the wife, but never told the wife to love the husband (Ephesians 5:25). She obviously responds to the love given to her.

Haven't you noticed that the man who is more attentive to a woman needs and blesses her with financial security, loving her extravagantly seem to keep a more pleasant relationship?

Please do not allow her to run amuck because you are good to her. Women can become a little bitchy so always keep your house in check. There is one king to a throne, two heads on anything is abnormal.

Lady's love to be pampered with hair dos, facials, nails manicured, feet pedicures, massages, nice cars and the ultimate shopping.

She loves to lay her beautiful body around a beautiful atmosphere. Can you imagine how beautiful everything was in the garden when Eve was placed there with Adam?

If God thought enough of her to place her in comfort and grandeur, who are you man to change Gods order? Anytime we change Gods order, it's messed up!

When men change Gods order, things get out of order. Look at your divorce rate. Look at broken marriages even among the stars, they have things but no unconditional love, Brother get with the program, create some stuff that will knock her off her feet. (*Pun intended*).

That's the position you want her in anyway, make it happen! She loves to receive and give!

Even if your dwelling place is not conducive for the greatest comfort, there is no excuse for not applying unconditional love, and trust this, that a woman will remain with you, help you to get it together once she feels the love.

Please remember if your atmosphere is somewhat challenging; she is in it with you (Denzel, Fences) and nobody will get with you during challenging times who weren't truly with you all the time.

And please take note; that two are better than one, because if the one falls he has the other to help him up.

The least you can do is prove to her that you love her unconditionally always. Make her feel that every day is Christmas and every night is New Year's Eve; she will always be there to help.

Obviously, she is not with you because of your wealth, you don't have any. So why is she there?

If it is not your money, and she can get laid anywhere; then it must be the need for your love.

For your love, I'll do anything!

There are many places on planet earth that we call paradise, but none can compare to Eden that God placed the man and woman in the beginning.

Just the thought of living in a place where God visited with his voice in the cool of the day had to be an overwhelming place of grandeur. The splendor, the beauty is beyond our imagination. But God placed the woman in such an atmosphere so that she would have comforts of life, security with the man.

A World of Marriages Out of Order

There is nowhere in the scriptures where she was told to till the ground; that's proof she is supposed to stay around the garden and please the man. That's the way God made her, that was the order set in the beginning and that should be the order of things for her now.

If man create a paradise for her and fill it with unconditional love where else can she go? If she abandons paradise, real love searching for love; the search has to lead her back to you. If she does not make it back to you, you are already set for the next one who deserves your atmosphere of joy and pleasure.

It is so unfortunate that the machinations of the devil, the frivolities of the world have deteriorated this moral fabric by leading men to prison, on drugs and homosexually.

It is not a man's fault if the woman allows the devil to trick her into separating herself from the security of man. Even in her foolishness man should never allow aberration from Gods order for man and woman. *Use godly knowledge (common sense) to reconcile the relationship. Bring her home.*

It is unconditional love that will bridge the gap between separation and reconciliation.

Some women don't want anything and don't desire to see you with anything. Always remember you cannot run a mule in the Kentucky derby.

If she doesn't appreciate paradise, unconditional love she has diamonds in her back, she look better going than she does coming. There are bigger fish in the sea that has never been caught.

It was during biblical times God proved his love for Israel by commanding his prophet Hosea to marry Gomer a harlot who separated herself from him. However, Hosea was compelled by God to find her and take her home. It was unconditional love that turned separation into reconciliation. Although Gomer was a whore who had gone astray it was unconditional love that looked beyond her faults and saw her needs.

The Power of Love

> *"Charity beareth all things, believeth all things, hopeth all things, endureth all things and it never fails." 1 Corinthians 13: 7-8a*

Charity is unconditional love that bears all things. This type of love forgives the woman whose affections at one time were for another lover. When Hosea found his wife, I doubt if she was in Sunday school, after all she was a whore.

Some of you may think that it's a fool who will take a woman back after she has done infidelity. It is the fool who thinks his woman has never had the proclivity to do it.

It's a necessity for man to feed the woman's mind so that she adjusts to the mental leading of him. It is the mind that needs to be comforted. The woman is emotional and in her mind, she does not enjoy being excluded all the time.

"The mind," says James Allen, "is like a garden, whether cultivated or neglected every seed will grow after its own kind."

If you allow seeds of loneliness, doubt to plant in her mind they will grow and she has nothing but negative seeds to feed on.

Let's do the opposite feed her thoughts with care, loves, self-esteem, security etc, etc. (see how easy that was).

Chapter Three

Please sir, understand that your woman for the first time in life has found strength, admiration and trust in you. Why should she not desire to be a part of you when she came from you?

She is still a woman and when she is tired of manly things she will get to herself and do girlish things apart from you, like read a book, look at fashion magazines, paint her nails. Always give her space.

Excluding her from sports or activities that you enjoy is one of the worse things a man can do. Some women desire to be a part of you whether she understands the game or not. Do not force what you enjoy with the fellows on her but expose her to it. If the sports event appeals to her she will take the initiative to learn and enjoy it with you sometimes.

The man whose wife became a sports caster is laughing all the way to the bank; and is ecstatic that he allowed her to be exposed to the game!

You may have gotten use to her but don't take her for granted. She is still a human being. And humans must interact sociably with other humans at some time or another. Suggest that she dresses up in your favorite dress take her out to dinner or wherever you suggest.

Most women don't want to answer questions, but told what to do. Some women love to be pretty and express their beauty while out with you. (WOW! That rhymes).

It takes very little time to read the newspaper or google to find out what's happening in the theater or the movies. Find a five-star hotel that houses a quiet lounge and sit with her for a couple of hours just to chat over a glass of wine or a cup of tea.

Learn to appeal to the woman's intellect. It takes very little effort to learn the title of a couple of classical songs if it's nothing but Beethoven fifth. You should always know the names of a couple of fine wines such as Louis Jadot Beaujolais, Pinot Grigio; even if you don't drink.

Chapter Three

Learn about fine artwork and the originators of them. (Claude Monet, Paul Gauguin, Pierre-Auguste Renoir) just to name a few for the sake of conversation.

Women admire the intelligent mind, why do you think they are attracted to Denzel.

Most woman need to feel that someone intellectually sound is leading her; intellect coupled with unconditional love will hold her interest. Why do you think most women acquiesce to men who are knowledgeable?

Nobody wants a dummy but a ventriloquist.

Sharpen your vocabulary with a few words that will stun her from time to time; stay abreast of current events and always be prepared to expound on social and world issues.

(Tell her baby you don't have to be ambiguous concerning my love for you, when you are alone with her "I don't know if I'm in a garden or on a crowded avenue, darling I only have eyes for you", be her lover).

Keep some power scriptures in your spirit to encourage her and strengthen her spirit, because the spiritual is the parent for the natural!

Give her your full attention and tell her how much she means to you and never be afraid to let her know you need her.

She will continue her desire to do everything she can to satisfy you, keep excitement in the relationship.

Hold her hand, look her in the eyes and tell her you desire to pray that she is always in good health. Lay your hand on her breast gently and pray that she never gets breast cancer.

Learn how to delineate in her mind romantic places you desire to vacation with her, then take her home and show her an evening she will never forget. It's always bubbles in the tub, scented oils, foot massages, back massages and spontaneous foreplay.

Chapter Three

Always put the icing on the cake. The evening is not complete without it. Also remember the same thing that's in the crumb is in the cake. A little bit of love goes along way with a woman when there is not enough time for the full evening of quality time.

Sex is just the icing on the cake. There should be something that sparks her intellect after you get out of bed and when she is away from you. Make it difficult for the next guy who may be better looking more financially secure than you to get her full attention.

There will always be another person who is more handsome with a more expensive automobile, more money than you. But is he a better lover?

Does he have the unconditional love in him?

It is the love, intellect that conquers her emotions! And money does answer all things.

Remember the first man Adam had the intelligence to name every animal in the garden.

This had to be mind boggling to Eve. The queen of Sheba fell in love with King Solomon because of his intellect to the point that she gave him of her treasures and of herself.

We are appalled at ignorant people who appear in movies, but we are in awe of people who appear to have intellect and knowledge.

Another man may appeal to her one way but does he appeal to all her senses as you do? Some woman will leave money, good looks for wisdom and unconditional love. Don't play her cheap; she will help you get money if the potential is there. If you will notice I said a woman! There is a difference between a gold digger and a woman.

Why do you think some women leave much to live with someone who has less?

One of the richest women in the world Christina Onassis, who was not considered to be a very attractive woman; went to Russia, found a manager of an apartment and married him because she was seeking love.

It was also printed that she paid two hundred thousand dollars to a man to make love to her and died a lonely woman because she never found unconditional love.

The Mind is a Terrible Thing to Waste.

The thought of leaving home begins in the mind of the woman. If you're constantly on her mind it doesn't matter if the situation changes. If you are in her head she will come home and will be glad to be there.

If I got your mind you will be glad to be wherever I am. It's relatively easy to control the woman's temperature; just be the thermostat of her mental state, which interacts with her emotional state; this is accomplished by unconditional love.

Don't expect ignorant woman to understand this discourse. The first thing they will say, "ain't no man gon control me", but they work for a boss who let them off the plantation on Friday, pay them just enough to survive until Tuesday in the ghetto, buy hair and booze and report back to the plantation on Monday.

Whenever she ceases to think like her man and for her man there is trouble in the camp. The two should be one, although the woman is an individual who thinks like her man and for her man, patterns herself in many instances like her man, she is his reflection.

When someone is in your corner; they don't think for another corner. They should think against the other corner that is competing against you.

In the boxing game, everyone in your corner is excited about you being the champ. When Ali was champ, Angelo Dundee and all his people had to think like him to help him.

The payday was greater when Ali won. That's why it's critical to keep that good woman in your corner and just as important for her to realize that she should remain there.

Two are better than one, because if one fall they have their partner to pick them up.

Chapter Three

Even if you lose a few of life's battles she will hang in the corner where she feels loved.

I remember when I was in the street life one of my girls was accosted by another pimp, he asks her why are you out here working hard for a guy who has one leg? She said daddy that made me work harder to get you plenty of money."

When a woman feels loved she can't be aberrated from the plans you have for her even if you are blind or in a wheel chair.

Haven't you noticed that the nursing profession began with women?

A woman is a remarkable creature; she will bathe your wounds, will clean you up, and will carry the weight until you regain your strength. During your weakest moments in life never lose the ability to show the woman love.

If you have someone who will bandage, bathe, clean, cook and serve you while you are down, the least you can do is lift up her spirit with unconditional love!

Four

LOSE YOUR MANHOOD, LOSE YOUR WOMAN!

Never lose the mystique and respect she has for you!

She respects you enough to always consider your leadership role in her life, and will assist you diligently with your goals and visions for her life.

As you lead in strength, she follows in strength, and there is no failure in you in her sight. Once the mystery of a movie is solved or revealed the show is over.

Never allow the woman to completely know every move, every emotion, and every thought about you. The wise King says, "Give not thy strength unto women, or thy ways to that which destroy Kings". Wise King Solomon warns us to keep the respect and the mystique alive by allowing yourself to not get too familiar with your own mate. (much *strategy needed*).

Don't ever compromise your principals as a man for the rudeness of a woman. Keep peace in your home by keeping disrespect in check.

Familiarity breeds contempt!

To breed is to produce; contempt is the act of despising, lack of respect or reverence for something.

When one is found in contempt of court they have lost the respect of the judge who is over the courtroom. Never allow a woman to lose respect for your leadership ability in her life.

Another wise man warns us, *"Keep the doors of your mouth from her that lieth in your bosom."*

You cannot allow your mate to know everything about you. It's not deliberate deceit, you must use subterfuge in some situations, especially if it will cause you to lose something that's valuable to you such as a wife.

Abraham was deceptive so that he would not lose his wife Sarah. Honesty is the best policy but don't be an honest fool! Never! Never!

Tell your woman you were not conversant with another woman, even if you are suspect in the act, *"baby that was not me!"*

Somethings are better not said anyway.

A client told me he told his wife he had an affair with another woman and she left him for another woman. Now there is a dysfunctional situation in his life he could have avoided by not being an honest fool.

I don't blame her. He would still have his wife if he had used discretion and kept his mouth shut. In other words, don't allow the woman to figure you out completely.

Have you ever awakened out of sleep and found your sweet thing looking at you?

She was thinking while you were sleeping and trying to figure you out. Many times, before the first date men think they saw the woman first and that he caught the woman.

But I've found out many times the woman saw you long before you saw her. And the only reason she caught your eye is because she put herself in position for you to see her.

There is a pretty woman in the bible named Esther who took her time preparing herself for three days, putting on her royal apparel and stood in the inner court of the king's house so that he could see her. And when he saw her he offered her half of the kingdom.

She positioned herself to attract the king, so that she could get what she wanted. She knew the livelihood of her nation was at stake.

When it concerns your livelihood for life, subterfuge can't hurt anything if it helps you keep a good woman.

Chapter Four

WOMEN ARE WISER THAN YOU THINK!

It is a prime case of the hunter being captured by the game. In human relationships, it's the game that is chasing the hunter; but the lady in the woman allows you to think you are chasing her.

The man who recognizes this paradox and keeps her chasing him, while at the same time pretends to chase her, knowing she is already captured is the boss of the love game. (Maybe you should read this again!) This is some heavy stuff, worthy of all acceptation. Love her but allow her a sense of freedom. I think it was Sting that sang, *"If you love somebody set them free."*

The sense of freedom in loving, draws her closer to you because it was not her intention to be free when she fell for you. She desired to be caught and kept. If you can stop her you can cop her. Master the art of keeping the chase going, she loves it.

Never allow her to really catch up with you.

No Fun When The Rabbit Gets The Gun!

Once your masculinity is consumed by femininity, forget about it! Bada boom! Bada bing!

Keep her thinking of you only. Once she knows everything about you she may just lose interest in you. Once the mountain is conquered the climber usually looks for another that's more challenging.

If somehow you have lost the respect of your woman prepare for the worst and hope for the better. Be open and honest with yourself because nine times out of ten the imputation of the matter is with you.

Examine yourself and attempt to make lemonade out of the lemon you created. Your real strength will depend on the unconditional love applied to the relationship. *pray it is not too late!*

When it becomes impossible to rekindle the fire, you will know it, move on with your life, there are bigger fish in the sea that has never been caught.

Do not waste time trying to make chicken soup out of chicken shit. Once unconditional love is totally rejected it's over!

Lust Hurts but Love Heals

Honesty is the best policy but you could suffer consequences.

Be honest with each other, and admit when it's over; it's just over and if you have become attracted to someone else, admit it carefully and go on with your life. (This can become a very hairy situation).

This is not the most comfortable situation for either party especially if one party is a jealous fool living in lust and not love. Lust can cause violence, where love covers a multitude of sin.

As I reiterate this is a very volatile situation, work your way out, be real smooth about the move, never abruptly drop the relationship with a sudden impact. There is nothing worse than a woman scorn!

The honest approach between man and woman to separate who are also lovers will simmer into friendship until intimacy and reconciliation is returned into the relationship.

No one enjoys the thought of an intimate lover giving what was once his or her stuff to someone else. But you cannot control another's emotions if they have decided to go elsewhere.

If someone else has her interest she is going to sneak with or without your consent.

Be a man, embolden her journey and remain in control by letting her go with love. You are out of control when you apply rage and violence to the game. Nothing and nobody is so significant you should kill or fight over them.

> *Fear will cause her to stray; love and respect will cause her to stay.*

Chapter Four

Unconditional love will wait patiently until she returns and if she doesn't show up, real love wishes her well.

Attraction is a natural propensity, someone reaches out and someone else reached back, and sometimes friendship cultivates into relationship that causes unfaithfulness.

Should the woman be stoned for her infidelity? Or do we use our energy and run to another lover ourselves? Use your energy to cultivate the friendship, relationship with her she is seeking elsewhere.

There is no resistance against persistence, but there is resistance against violence.

Violence invites too many outside forces. Firstly, it affects the children if there are any. It causes the law to enter your personal life. It awakens your neighbors to your personal business, when you can apply unconditional love to the situation that begs for peace, patience and persistence.

Let he who has not been attracted to another woman cast the first stone.

Charity believes all things.

Do not believe everything a woman say. But believe you can create good out of bad. That's all God does with all of us. He takes nothing and makes something.

If the woman is deemed no good in your sight because of her bitchy ways, then believe you can love her spite of herself into a complete lady.

If she doesn't make the cut, you did your best, because you believed in her when she did not believe in herself. God loved us when we did not love ourselves. She failed God; you did not because you did the will of God when you loved her unconditionally.

Charity hopes in all things; this type of unconditional love can say good-bye and at the same time keep hope alive. Pertaining to relationship, why should we invest twenty years of our lives in a woman give up on her because she decided to try another relationship? (*I'll be dog gone*)!

Why not continue to keep hope alive in the relationship, at the same time press for a love so great that you are free enough on the inside to free her on the outside from any place that she desires to be; even if it's not with you!

Continue to be her friend. It is easier said than done to remain and contain friendship with an ex-lover, but with unconditional love it can be accomplished.

It's like receiving bad news that helps you; it may be the worst day of your life but the best day at the same time.

There is a power in the man who loves unconditionally allowing him to say goodbye, remain friends with the woman who hurt him and have hope in the return of the love he has applied in the past. If the relationship moves from friendship and lover to friendship only, you are still victorious. Think of winning never losing.

Man is always in control if he loves.

Christ never stopped loving those who denied or betrayed him and was assured of their return.

He even called Judas friend when Judas gave him the kiss of death. While hanging from the cross Christ remained in control, "Father forgive them for they know not what they do."

The very command for forgiveness upon those who was killing him was an act of unconditional love. After he arose from the dead he told Mary, "Go tell my brethren and Peter," the one who denied him to meet him in Galilee; was also an act of unconditional love for a friend who denied him in time of trouble.

He received with open arms everyone who denied, betrayed and forsook him and never mentioned the past. Let this be a lesson to the unconditional lover.

Unconditional love endures all things. The principal behind this love is to play the hand that's dealt you and never change your expression when the cards are not in your favor.

Chapter Four

In the game of spades the Joker is your trump card. If someone spreads four Aces thinking they won the game, you can play the Joker and beat them out. Unconditional love is your trump card; hold it close to your bosom.

The man who loves his woman can know the details of the deception and have compassion on the deceiver. This lover can pray for the woman who left him, for the man she left him for. Through unconditional love you can find peace in a situation that has not been changed.

It is amazing what the human mind and heart can endure when it is steeped with the power of unconditional love.

> *Charity never fails. In all that you do to a man who loves unconditionally, his love will never fail you. He will always be your friend. You cannot upset him or dismay him. He loves you with the love of God because he is born of God. There is no failure in God's love. It passes all knowledge and covers a multitude of sin.*

Unauthorized Liberation

It is not Gods fault, the woman today has allowed sexual revolution to fool her into masculinizing herself with the feminist movement to liberate her from the security of man.

There is a distinct difference between feminism and femininity.

Feminism emphasizes dependence;
Femininity stress interdependence.

Feminism says I am woman;
Femininity says I am woman that desire a man.

Feminism has a sense of competition against man;
Femininity endorses co-operation with man.

Feminism increases marital discord;
While femininity increases marital accord.

Feminism emphasizes aggressive action;
Feminism emphasizes progressive action.

The feminist is an arrogant woman;
The feminine is an elegant woman.

The feminist emphasizes woman's rights;
Femininity emphasizes being the right woman.

And it's not your fault, the lover is so depraved in his thinking that he's blind concerning your value to him and what an asset you are.

You are the essence of femininity, the epitome of womanhood, the personification of female, the embodiment of she-ism, the manifestation of man. For you were taken out of man, you belong to man, to be in relationship with man.

*The man is emboldened to care for you
and secure your life.*

Jesus Christ is then glorified and magnified in the man who cares enough for his woman to sacrifice his life to give her a better life. Take care of her as Christ does for his bride the church. But of course, most men are not on their job. Some men are trying to secure another man's house while his home is falling apart.

If I'm the head of my house I have the authority to control the temperature there. I can never allow my wife to get cold *(If you get my meaning).*

A woman should never be allowed to even get lukewarm. A fire should burn in her heart always. Her desire should always be for her man. It is a sad commentary today that some men have dropped the ball to the point that some women desire another woman. How can these things be?

Women are moody and sometimes they are into their own world and that's O.K.; because everybody needs his/her own space sometimes. There is a way to get along with a woman no matter the mood! The first thing a man must learn to do is discern her body language, love her faults and shortcomings; the rest of her is easy to love.

Opinion

I imagine that this is the tactic the devil uses to lure the natural woman into the arms of a lesbian. It is easy for the lesbian to capture the woman because she is a woman herself and know the faults and weaknesses of another. And I believe she loves the faults and shortcomings of the damsel in destress and fulfills the void that the man neglects (end).

Wives submit to your own husbands in everything!

Now sweetheart everything is everything! The law of love is to love thy neighbor as thy self. *Well your mate is a little closer than your neighbor I hope!*

And of course, it is an anthropomorphism to ascribe God to having human form; but if He needed a bath would you run his bath water? Would you deny Him one second of your love? Would you decorate Gods table and place his meal beautifully on the table? Well your husband or significant other is made in the likeness of God.

Undefiled Bed

The bedroom is probably the most lived inn room in the home. The room gets junky enough without you defiling it with outside demons.

Man is the head of the home and is the lover in the relationship. Haven't you noticed the woman is relatively easy to satisfy? She will eat hamburgers or go with you to the steak house.

Many times, you will pop the question, honey what do you want to eat or where do you want to go, or what movie do you want to see? And she will respond by saying, it is up to you, because she depends on you leading her as head of the house and the lover, who she expects to create so strong an atmosphere this is the place she desires to be.

Create an atmosphere especially in the bedroom, give her reasons for being there other than for sleeping.

There is nothing wrong or feminine if a man finds sweet odors, pillows of silk and satin for his woman to smell and relax on for comfort and pleasure. The problem is most men care more for dressing up their cars and give little attention to the bedroom. This concept is O.k. However, if you live by yourself and in your car.

"Marriage is honorable in all and the bed undefiled."
Hebrews 13:4

Where is your camera? How exciting it is for her to pose privately and dance to soft music in the bedroom; you are not in church, I repeat; you are not in church; there is a time and place for everything.

Play an old fashion love song!

Complete body massages, bubble baths, rose petals for her to lie on are in order in your private chamber. If Adam and Eve danced they darned very little or it was in the nude. *It takes two to tango!*

Keep the relationship exciting!

After the baths give her massages to release all stress so that she can relax her mind and concentrate solely on you. Purchase the Victoria Secret you desire her to wear while dancing or modeling for you.

Give her nice gifts, place flowers on the nightstand or a meaningful card on the pillow before she enters your chambers. Know her favorite candies, give them to her now and then; she just may enjoy it with you. This enhances love and lovemaking.

> *"Let her breast satisfy thee always; and be thou ravished always with her love." Proverbs 5: 19b*

Love her extravagantly! Does not God show extravagant love to us? The difference is He operates in the spiritual, but gave us all we need to operate in the natural, use it or lose it.

Saved brothers, please learn to pull out more than your bible in the bedroom; *"be thou ravished with her love."*

> ***You are supposed to be overjoyed,***
> ***Bursting with happiness.***
> ***On top of the world.***
> ***Enchanted.***
> ***High and freaked out.***
> ***In a transport of delight.***
> ***Carried away.***
> ***Beside oneself with joy.***
> ***In paradise.***
> ***On cloud nine.***

Chapter Four

Lose yourself in lovemaking; be carried away with her love. Enjoy her breast always. Someone said they are fun bags, have fun with her and she will have fun with you.

Sex is not spiritual. It's kinky, raw, down and dirty. Some people will often say, "I had sex in the spirit." Please explain to me how you did that!

If the sister is spiritual she should reflect as such among society; but allowed to relax and be who she wants to be in the bedroom.

The thrill, the satisfaction, the excitement in sexual intercourse is the same for women in the church as it is for women outside of the church. Just because you are in the church the man does not insert his penis quoting the Lord's prayer or in any foolish fashion. You do not have sex singing Amazing Grace!

An orgasm is an orgasm for all women.

The same oral copulation the women in the world perform is the same as the church woman.

The man in the world applies foreplay to the same areas as the deacon or the preacher.

As a matter of fact, some of the church women should begin some lessons in lap dancing and some other kinky stuff, so they can keep a husband from looking around in the choir.

Hang off the chandeliers or stand on top of your head if you want too. Put up your degree and bring out your thongs.

Bust out with some Victoria Secret or some other stuff and drive him out of his mind thinking only of you. If he's taken to the crazy house make sure he is calling out your name.

Give him the kind of love that will cause him to howl at the moon at night, and search for you in the daytime with a flashlight.

Please be a tramp in the bedroom if you desire too. Sexual attraction is to be acted out not totally understood. You are doing nothing wrong by being attracted to each other, and parts of each other's body.

Chapter Four

Don't let some super religious people fool you. Save your marriage and your relationships. Some of them are doing more than you can imagine.

God is big enough to allow you to enjoy your sex life and keep you as his child. God don't expect you to love him in the same fashion as your mate. That's impossible, because God is spirit who gave us mind body, sexual organs, emotions, passions, spirit and each other to enjoy.

Man should not rest until an atmosphere is created, the woman desires.

Just think of the lips, hips, and fingertips that's waiting to give you pleasure. She is worth preparing for.

> *"A bundle of myrrh is my well beloved unto me; he shall lie all night betwixt my breasts."*
> Song of Songs 1:13

The woman desires the man smell good always, especially while making love. Experiment with different fragrances until you get the right one for your body chemistry.

If you have good hygiene the natural smell is an aphrodisiac and can be as a bundle of myrrh to the woman. Myrrh is an aromatic gum resin from several trees and shrubs of the genus Commiphoro of India, Arabia, and Eastern Africa, used in perfume and incense.

The oil called musk attempts to capture the natural odor of a human but there is nothing on the market named funk. (Don't even try it)!

Before you lay your head between her breasts find a soft smelling fragrance for your head or hair that will appeal to the senses of the woman.

Kiss her breast gently until she is relaxed and begins to rub your face; head or other parts of your anatomy. Let her breast satisfy you always. Gently kiss all around them before you reach the main point. (Enjoy the whole meal before desert).

It is critical the man maintain a habit for being well groomed. When you get your hair cut, get your nails manicured and feet pedicures; there is nothing wrong with being cured all over. What

Chapter Four

kind of woman desires nasty nails inside of her vagina?

And who in their right mind desires deliberate smelly feet or bad breath.

Woman, don't put your man away if he is not well groomed; teach him concerning the things you love in a man. Men, take heed to the woman's advice to better the relationship.

Drop your pride and get well-groomed, she will give you more reason to drop your pants.

"Behold thou art fair, my love beholds, thou art fair; thou hast dove eyes." Song of Songs 1:15

It is always appropriate to compliment a woman concerning her beauty while making love. If you will notice the lover repeated himself (thou art fair, my love beholds thou art fair) the lover put emphasis on the beauty of the woman. Fair means good to look upon, (*easy on the eye*) compliment her for that.

It is the significant thing to do; slow down; take it easy in the very act of lovemaking and compliment her on her beauty.

This is characteristic of a true lover. It intimates a true virtue you are interested in making love and not just have sex. Most men think only of themselves in the act of having sex. Every man has a penis, but does every man know how to use it.

Practice the art of lovemaking. It also prolongs the climax; which is in your favor. The art of lovemaking is to control the mind and the body will follow.

Compliment her on the shape of her lips: the beauty of her eyes, the smell of her hair. The woman desires to have something verbal in her ear while receiving what you are sending physically.

(The degree of verbal language is up to the lover).

Don't talk too much; but feel her out with a sexy word or two and see how she reacts. Most

Chapter Four

woman desire sensual talk while in the act of intercourse, some will tell you, *(talk dirty to me)*.

Behold means look! Apparently, there were mirrors around the bed.

"Thou art fair, my beloved, and yea, pleasant: also, our bed is green." Song of Songs 1:16

Solomon was the richest man on earth during his time with seven hundred wives and three hundred concubines. I'm sure some of them were from Egypt where mirrors were originated. I'm more than sure that one of them was freaky enough to request mirrors around the bed.

It is huge to put more emphasis on the atmosphere of the room, the bed on which the main event is taking place.

Most women love mirrors, they love to pose in front of a camera. Everybody needs his or her fifteen minutes on stage. Give her the stage: let her be the star. Allow her to act out all her fantasies.

You can begin your interview on the casting couch before moving to the bedroom. Build her up to act out her starring role; you just sit back direct and enjoy the show.

You have never received love or lovemaking until you allow the woman to relax and be herself from all her hang-ups and inhibitions.

Never dim the lights in her heart, or take her off stage: keep her in the spotlight of your heart always. And please don't limit yourself to the bedroom. She is well able to give you a grand performance in other places.

Use chairs, bathrooms, the beach and any other means necessary leading up to the main event. The kitchen is always a good place to begin foreplay. There are several practices and games played before you get to the championship.

Your bedroom must be creatively colorful, scented with exotic odors. Hear me now, the woman will easily tire from the usual bim - bam- thank –u –mam!

Don't be tolerated be celebrated!

Create an atmosphere where the woman desires to be with you only, will run to get to you when she is away from you.

Opinion

Millions of women flock to clubs every weekend, take flights, flock to beaches to tan, shop for sexy clothes to wear to get your attention, they spend millions for hair do's nails, and they exercise to trim themselves to please a man. They desire to please, so create the atmosphere for pleasure she will flock to you.

There is a reason why women flock to men in the world, male stripper clubs, pay them for pleasure and excitement. Some women have suffered abuse because of false love. How far do you think she will go with you if you are kind to her and show her unconditional love?

Defiled Bed

You are mendacious to yourself if you think you can bring a stranger into your bedroom and your woman is not affected by it. When you bring a strange woman's spirit into that sacred, intimate place; you bring whatever spirits the strange woman possesses. This defiles your bed.

Let's say the strange woman is very promiscuous and is sleeping around with other lovers. This can be very pernicious to your personal relationship. You can destroy everything you built up that's personal and pleasurable between the two of you, and all the effort you put into keeping her to yourself.

It may cause your lover to desire a third party and you wonder why. You brought that spirit into your mix, your bed is now defiled. And unless you can satisfy the defilement: which is wrong in the sight of God; you now have a woman who is unhappy because you are not able to comply.

And if you bring another spirit into your bedroom and it is strong enough and she is weak enough she will adhere to the strongest spirit.

Her spirit may be willing to do right by you; but the flesh is weak.

Chapter Four

And now Dr. Frankenstein you have just created a monster who will turn on you. She was once satisfied in your presence and the atmosphere you created, now she is frustrated and unhappy with you; her desire is the desire of the outside spirit you brought into your relationship.

It is possible she now desires more than one man; she may also acquire an appetite for a woman. Or it's possible to bring home a murdering spirit.

Commentary

There is nothing worse than an unhappy woman in your life. Wise King Solomon says, and I quote from Proverbs 25: 24, *"It's better to dwell in the corner of the housetop than with a brawling woman in a wide house."*

It is better she's happy in that one cozy room full of the atmosphere for love, lovemaking than live in a mansion full of sorrow. A woman would rather be in one room where she feels a cathedral of love, than live in a cathedral not feeling loved at all.

She will leave riches (Diana left Prince Charles), if they are not loved. I've heard women say, "Lie to me, say you love me even if you don't mean it; lie to me, say that you do." That's how important love is to some women.

Men have forced women into social independence, lesbianism, sex shops to find pleasure because man in many instances have failed the natural methodology to sustain the woman's desire; to genuinely love them unconditionally.

THE SERIOUS DOCTOR EXAMINES THE WHOLE BODY

There are so many nerves, feelings and systems that make up the human anatomy. We have muscle systems, nerve systems, a vertebral column, skeletal system, vascular and viscera system, etc, etc. We have so many emotions and passions inside these nerves and systems.

Chapter Four

Every strand of a woman's hair; is connected to nerves or feelings. Everything on her body is connected to something that will either cause her pleasure or pain. It's up to you to relax her and find out what causes her to feel pain or pleasure. When you find the pleasure places work with it until....

It's as if you stumbled upon a pearl that's precious, keep working in the same place there just may be more to come, or she may cum more.

You will find many pleasure places; that will not only cause her to feel as if she is in ecstasy; but will also cause her to develop a desire for you beyond your imagination. You must tap into those spots, other men never thought to explore.

Remember every woman is different, but is the same when it comes to love, they like different stuff, but they all need satisfaction; excite her by exploring areas of satisfaction.

Women love touching and pleasure.

If you will give attention to your woman, you won't have time to worry about another, spend time learning your woman and what really turns her on. There is more to a woman than just pumping up and down now and then.

A serious doctor can talk to his patient on the phone and diagnose what she need. Sometimes before you make your house call, hold an examination on the phone.

Your woman should be able to talk to you on the phone and conclude she desires you physically before you connect. You should captivate her mind to the point if you are miles away she can reach some of the same results as if you were in bed with her.

Expert Opinion

> *"If you have not firstly penetrated her mind causing her to acclimatize her thoughts and body to your thoughts until she is intoxicated from your sexual verbosity then you are not in control of the relationship." Al Calvert*

Chapter Four

Maintain excitement in the relationship; and keep a burning desire in the woman always. Reason being; there are mood swings and turn-offs to the woman. Sometimes a phone call can determine what kind of mood she is in before going home.

Take a gift home to enhance her mood.

When company comes over it is a joy they thought enough of you to bring something besides themselves. It is not so much the gift as it is the thought. Don't get too familiar with your mate, keep it exciting by inviting yourself home as company sometimes and take something home with you beside yourself.

"Never allow the novelty of the relationship to wear off."

Although the woman loves you, she is still a human being, and one of the worst things in the world to another human; is to be boring. Keep it tight and she will keep it right.

Never abrogate the ability to court your mate.

> *"Life is a big game; the one who has the most fun wins."*

A kind word before going home may determine what's in store for you and the outcome of the evening. A few dollars in a card arouses the senses in a woman. It excites her just as it excites you.

> *Money pleases her just as it pleases you!*

Some of you have spent money on things and didn't get anything back, learn to give the woman some money and she will freely give up the honey.

Two Pleasures at One Time

Usually when they have an appetite for dinner they have an appetite for love.

Talk softly to her at dinner, explain that eating with her is a very pleasurable experience. But the dinner is secondary to the most pleasurable experience, which is sharing it with her. Make her feel the meal is enjoyed only because she is with you.

Make her feel that eating with her gives you a chance to share in two of the most pleasurable experiences at the same time, looking at her while enjoying the meal.

A lady told me once that when the man blessed the food before they began to eat it turned her on. She said, "It excited her when the man bowed his head to bless God before eating." So always show God reverence in the presence of the woman. What do you have to lose?

We can lust after a woman because she is appealing to our flesh, but what's going to happen on those days when she doesn't look so good or if she is ill for a while. It takes unconditional love to love the unlovable. If your mate is diagnosed with cancer it will take unconditional love to care for her for better or for worse, in sickness and in health.

Fall in love with her faults and shortcomings, be her friend. If she shops for hours and don't buy anything so what? You watched the game for hours and your team lost.

Body Language

Never and I mean never take a woman for granted. They are emotional creatures, subject to change at the drop of a hat. It will do you justly to painstakingly watch her body language. You can make the wrong move at the wrong time and blow the whole evening. You should not be touchy, feely when she just wants to vent. They love to talk then touch; then it is time to get closer to her.

You should never rush a woman to have sex; that only happens in the movies and on the Soaps. Remember what's inside your pants is just as important to her as what's underneath her dress. The key is to make her starve for pleasure.

And trust this, "if a woman is in heat for you she will always reach for the meat from you."

Chapter Four

This is a good time to hold an examination on parts of her body that will bring her to the height of sexual satisfaction without penetrating her. Penetration is the ultimate for her. Hold out for as long as possible before going to the mountaintop with her. *Learn to hold your piece!*

I don't know much about mountain climbing, but it is common sense you began at the bottom before going to the top. Also, there is much preparation before climbing a mountain.

The initial act of sexual intercourse is spontaneous most of the time. However, the ultimate goals are, each party reach the top and remain there in each sexual act. It's not pleasing all the time for one to remain mountain high and the other is not.

Beforehand the initial act should always be enhanced and no one should ever be let down; this takes preparation. (*It's called foreplay*). Foreplay should never be taken lightly. You should spend as much time as possible learning the parts on her body that will cause her to make a joyful noise.

A woman's feet are a very serious issue with her and it should be with you also. Why do you think they get pedicures, polish their toes with different colors?

They want you to acquire a fetish for them. Some women will have surgery on their feet to make themselves attractive for you. Every part of her body, every fiber of her being is to be examined and explored for your pleasure.

Most women with pretty feet love for the man to massage them and…

Women are somewhat strange, sometimes-strange things turn them on. Just follow the body language while holding the examination, the body will tell you whether it is pain to her or pleasure. A woman will let you know what she enjoys, if she is enjoying herself.

Five

SOME BONES TO SUCK ON

The Spontaneous Woman

It is the writer's opinion the spontaneous woman or Nymph is the most exciting woman.

She may try anything at any time; it's all good. It's wise to allow her to get out of control while controlling the energy, simultaneously satisfying her. Because of her sensual desires never allow her to feel she is less than pleasurable in her approach. The spontaneous woman is a great companion and joy to socialize with.

After all, most men desire their mate reach the level of a super lover.

So why make her feel as if she is less than a woman because she likes what she likes, if you like it enough to do it with her then what is that saying about you?

When a man loves this woman, he causes her to feel loved and appreciated, will not degrade her for her passions, sexual longevity, methods of pleasing during the initial act. *Allow her to be herself!*

It is in the man and not in the land to control the atmosphere of this certain burst of heated passion expressed to you, or you will find yourself in a quickie situation and she's still not satisfied. It is here where the key to control is huge. Control penetration for as long as possible. Learn to love the woman and make love instead of just having sex.

> *Most women have had sex, but most of them are starving for someone to make love.*

Learn to love them after the lovemaking have become reticent. There is a plethora of things to do to show your love after the act is over, one is to give her a birdbath (wash certain private parts) while she is still in bed and talk dirty to her.

Never inadvertently do things for the woman but carefully chose things that turn her on more and more. When a man loves this woman, he will go with the flow of excitement.

"Since she is the only being on planet earth who's suitable for man, the same consciousness as a man then she should be satisfied at all times."

The more she is satisfied the more she will satisfy you. If you are man you need satisfaction from wo-man.

The Unhappy Woman

How did we grow so far apart? Why did she discontinue her aggressiveness toward me? Suddenly, she is not freaky anymore. I wonder why we don't do the things we use to do?

There should be nothing enigmatic concerning her sudden shift of attention toward you; if you have slacked up on your attention toward her. Remember she reciprocates to the proportion of love she has received. If you have put nothing in you can take nothing out.

Women go through body changes, crises later in life with P.M.S; hot flashes and all, but at the same time they desire to be loved, they desire to be made love to.

When a woman is going through body changes it does not necessarily mean she is involved with another man: It has nothing to do with another man or she's unhappy. It's the way it is. This is another case where it's significant the man has fallen in love with the woman faults and shortcomings.

How many men have lost good women because they did not have patience enough with the woman when she was simply going through mood swings or body change? It had nothing to do with her being unhappy in the relationship; she was just being herself, doing the best she could at the time.

During those critical times in her life, let her alone for she has done what she could with what she's got. Give her a little time, she'll surprise you with some unforgettable evenings.

The key is to remember she was going through and not to stay.

The unhappy woman usually finds comfort in talking to someone else because she is ignored at home. She just wanted someone to converse with and it was you. Once again if you allow the only conscious being on planet earth who is suitable for you; can satisfy you to get cold on you; then the imputation of the matter is on you.

You should have noticed by now her body language intensely; vociferously crying out for more attention, but you have allowed the devil to place an obstinate attitude in your heart, have become pertinacious; ignoring the cry from the only conscious mate you have on this planet.

Your way out is to draw from the well that never runs dry, unconditional love. Now you must go through the pain of loving her backsliding mental state that, *"you just don't care anymore."* And bring her back from insecurity to security and trust in you.

Wise King Solomon says, *"there is nothing worse than a woman scorn, it is better for a man to live in the corner of a rooftop."*

Before unhappiness sets into the heart and mind of a woman; the man must counter all negatives; insecurities, assuring her you love her, and she is the apple of your eye. The same thing it took to catch her is the same thing it will take to keep her. Nobody desires to live confused, rejected, or miss-understood.

1. Confused, mistake for another to bring to ruin.
2. Rejected, refuse to hear, receive or admit, to throw back.
3. Misunderstood, fail to understand.

No human being desires to live under these conditions not even you.

Negative characteristics will exalt themselves in the heart of your mate if you don't apply positive unconditional love in its place.

We cannot assume everything is all right when in two or three weeks or even days, we have done nothing extra to satisfy. If life is lived by every second in the day, love and happiness can slowly abrogate itself at any second of the day. *Give no place to the negative.*

Especially if the negative is whispering sweet nothings in her ear and you are not.

Consider if you will the woman is a human being, she is delicate, feminine, emotional and she represents you. I would not want any parts of me unhappy, especially when she is preparing my food, taking care of my children.

When the woman feels constantly excoriated this could induce separation, after separation, divorce and divorce sometimes brings about dysfunction of the family for generations to come.

Why go through all this pain when you can deter it with love?

It's still Roses

She may get upset because you forgot to bring home some roses. She is worth the whole flower shop. She is a rose, just because the rose has a few thorns it continues to exude a sweet fragrance. No one in their right mind when picking a rose handles it so carelessly they forget about the thorns. The appearance of the thorns causes us to handle the rose with care.

*Liken the woman to the rose and
handle her thorns carefully.*

Handle her doubts, fears and concerns with love. Unconditional love is the significant thing. It will keep the woman running back to you.

Keep the main thing the main thing!

Happiness is not in the abundance of things. Most women have had other men to approach them with feeble attempts to buy their affection with things. If a woman is unhappy; things won't make her happy.

Chapter Five

Unconditional love comes first, then things!
It's more serious than you think!

Understand some women have been scared from their youth with deep psychological wounds from molestation, rape, abuse and battery. Some have trusted men who abused them early in life.

Some were robbed of the purity; and early beginnings of their idealistic minds, dropped like a hot potato. And you come home with a peck on the cheek and a pat on the butt demanding dinner and sex after you've hurt her feelings.

Without love you are just adding fuel to the fire.

Sure, the sex patches things up for a moment. But it takes more than band aids to heal a deep-rooted wound. To reach beyond the crust of all that psychological madness it takes a constant application of patience, understanding and unconditional love.

I repeat and will repeat it again, learn to fall in love with her shortcomings, her faults, be her best friend, the rest is easy.

All of us have something in us now that's not pleasing; originated in our childhood or early stages of our lives.

Now please sir: do not go probing and prying into old wounds to find out who raped your woman, where and how she was battered, who molested her, where and how long. *Let by gone be by gone!*

If she ever opens up to you, shares these pains with you, just listen; cry with her and hold her as if she is the last woman on planet earth.

Build up self-esteem, secure her insecurity's, never mention the conversation again. Don't hold these things against her; they are a part of her past life; negative things happen in everybody lives.

No matter how angry you become with her, never scorn her concerning personal information she shared with you about her past. She shared it because she trusted you; felt relaxed with you, strength from you; *never break this covenant!*

How would you like for someone to take a knife and continue to stab you in the same wound over and over? The significant thing is to recognize there is a problem and love her through it.

The Materialistic Woman

This woman is a very ambitious woman strong in nature and tender at heart.

The man who loves this woman must have patience, long suffering, endless trust for her. Be very patient with her, she will spend hours shopping and may not buy two much of anything.

If you are not careful your mind will play tricks on you, thinking she is with another man during the countless hours she is alone just window shopping or searching every clearance rack in Macy's looking for a bargain. Understand shopping is therapy for her.

It is not difficult to recognize the character of the materialistic woman; her closet is full of clothes with the tag still hanging on them. It is such a joy to date this woman, she will make you very proud to have her on your arms because she is the best-dressed woman wherever you take her.

Enjoy her breast always and be ravished with her love.

She is somewhat vain in character but her positive attributes override any of her negative disposition. She loves to model new garments for you to get your approval. You must constantly feed her ego. She is one of the greatest lovers on this planet. She is also spontaneous and full of surprises.

She is easy to love, very gentle and kind... The man who love this woman must get ready to travel and enjoy an exciting life of fun, pleasure because she is ready to vacation and shop in any parts of the world.

Chapter Five

Lost and Turned Out!

There are beautiful, wonderful, intelligent, talented single women who have experienced sex, but have been robbed of the opportunity to express themselves in serious relationships, due to male incompetency, or lack thereof.

Some of them were just walking a normal course of life; were very dis-appointed early in life and lost their zest for love. Many of them remained confused for many years.

Because someone who were too evil to consider the pain she would have to endure, imposed different negative acts upon her.

Some of these wonderful ladies were just hanging out with friends, innocently received a substance from a friend, experienced it, just to be a part of the set, and were duped into the allusion from the substance and joined group orgies.

Some were just walking a normal course of life, a relative who was lesbian robbed her of her heterosexual appetency, she remained confused for years wondering if I am man or woman.

Some went out to a club or concert because of loneliness and it was a natural proclivity; someone got her attention; they reached out and she reached back, fell in love with false promises and found herself prostituting.

In some cases, she was raped, molested or battered. But understand one thing when approaching this woman; she is a child of God and He desires that she is loved.

When a man loves this woman, he will look pass the ugliness of the deposits that have been placed in her by someone else, and pick her up out of the gutter where someone else left her in to die.

Because she has been lost and turned out, she must be found by a strong man who will love her and protect her unconditionally with patience until her break through from these negative shortcomings.

Once she has assurance, and the realization she is forgiven and respected, she will unite with you in strength; and there is nothing she would not do for you. I believe she will be a good wife, the greatest companion. She is not a loser because she has always had to fight her way out, she is not as bad as her situation because she got through it.

If the man can understand her past experiences only strengthen her; and through his help he can transform the negative into positive; she is the greatest friend, companion and lover ever. She is not afraid or inhibited, all that's required is the love and affection from the man who can look past her faults and see her needs.

Mary Magdalene in her past had suffered many things, but after she met Jesus who loved her despite her failures; she remained the best friend and servant to our Lord. She even washed his feet with her tears and dried them with her hair.

Once the lost is found, the turned out is turned in, she receives her healing and feels loved, she will be your best friend, there is nothing she won't do for you.

The Super Saint

The Supper saint in my opinion denies herself an essential part of the abundant life God intended for her. She has had one bad relationship and don't trust men anymore.

She has purposed in her heart, men are no good. Her judge mental attitude limits her altitude; now she looks upon the outward appearance of men and determines none of them are good enough for her.

She lives under the false pretense that spiritual love is all she need when in fact she is starving for paternal love. Her testimony is Jesus is all I need. Well this is all our testimony, but Jesus is the one who took her from man and gave her to man to be loved by man.

Her crutch is to wear long dresses, carry a bible bigger than anyone else's. She's in church every time the doors open and another part of her cover is she constantly speaks in tongues but may not speak to the man who she really admires.

Chapter Five

This is to cover up her desire, weakness as a woman who does desire a man, that's human nature. To say she doesn't desire a man is to say she's abnormal. It's normal and very much human to desire sexual satisfaction from the opposite sex.

God did not take away our sexuality or sensuality because his spirit is in us and we got saved.

When a man loves this woman, he loves her respecting her religiosity, but he must bring about some balance in her life; to have a good woman and one of the most sensual women on the planet.

She has stored up much and there is much to be released. Love her through the fanaticism, which is not a bad thing to be in her faith, but bring about a balance while abolishing all inhibitions.

Hopefully she will remain balanced, pray she doesn't move too far to the left. Her faithfulness will keep her from many of her demons. She will be too ashamed to pull up her dress in front of anyone except her husband. No guarantees but we hope so! Usually just as she is a super saint she will be a supper lover to her husband.

*"Marriage is honorable in all and the bed undefiled."
Hebrews 13:4*

When a man loves this woman, he will not attempt to change her love for her faith, this is not advisable, but share with her in her love for her faith. Remember she loves hard once she loves.

Slowly introduce her to games such as dominoes, scrabble and then strip poker, introduce her to sexy underwear you desire.

Make life fun for her outside of the church and in the bedroom; because the church is all she knows, this also is not a bad thing. It's a good thing because hopefully her faith has kept her decent for you.

Remember underneath all the speaking in tongues, hymns, long prayers and church programs—which is great because she is growing stronger in the faith—however she's still a woman and God says she is the weaker vessel (1 Peter 3:7). *She needs your unconditional love!*

The Church Prostitute

Usually she is one of two extremes, very quiet, un-noticed or very outgoing. Her sexual expertise is moving among respectful men in the church with temptation to justify her promiscuity. If he did it with me it must be all right. And in the interim of the temptation she will get her beg on for money. She is always losing her house or the car note is behind.

It is paradoxical but this woman is one of the kind-hearted women in the church while at the same time one of the kinkiest. When a man loves this woman, he is taking some risk because she is so unpredictable. He must be willing to love her, make love to her extravagantly, gently and extremely while remaining in the parameters of not indulging into lasciviousness.

It is essential she is brought into total submission in the bedroom and her time outside of the home is accounted for.

Be certain that you have captured her emotions.

She is a force to be reckoned with; to capture her emotions is to keep her satisfied sexually and monetarily. If she is ever caught in a fault, forgive her, love her as if she never did anything wrong. Because all she was looking for while away from you was love and money.

The Secular Woman

Everyone needs a renewed mind. However, without some spiritual change as the center of her life she wanders about attempting to appease herself with different lovers; searching for joy, happiness only one man can give. Much of her social life is spent in nightclubs or concerts. She desires to meet a man who will love her, help her out of debt; *debt that she has acquired while shopping for things she could not afford.*

If she catches a workingman she plays him as if he is a trick; but if she catches a dope boy she may have some respect until she figures out his weaknesses. Her whole method of measuring her

Chapter Five

value is between her legs and of course oral copulation.

The little child's dad who promised her the world, had sex, left them and never paid a dime in child support; this ordeal also has affected her attitude toward love.

She is a very strong woman because she has had to fend for herself in the streets all her life. Some of her self-esteem is lost because of the different men who have dropped her for one reason or another. Her front is fancy hairdos and skimpy clothes, tattoos and so on.

He who picks a rose must accept the thorns it bears.

When a man loves this woman, he should come with a sense of offering security for her and the children; and willing to give sacrificial love for her and his new family; because she has had many unsuccessful relationships that caused insecurity.

She will have a sense of insecurity for a while and will try to run things even your life. Nip this in the bud and get an understanding that she doesn't run anything over in the house but her shoes.

Give her a sense of responsibility but never show weakness to her dominant nature. Unconditional love, strength and power will bring her to the realization of who she is and what she is in your life.

Don't argue or fight her at any time because that's her past environment. Confusion will give her the opportunity to bring old wine into new wineskins.

She is operating under a bad spirit until you can bring her a new environment. She must be renewed in her mind and only your love and patience will get her there; when a man loves this woman.

The Professional Woman

She has spent most of her life in school and after graduate school has spent most of her time around a few stiff-necked professional men who was seeking their own careers.

Chapter Five

They didn't have time to give her the quality time and attention needed. This woman is sensual and starving for love and lovemaking.

She has gone on cruises, vacationed in the Islands, had an affair with a stranger who she never saw again in life and did not care to see; but did it and paid for it because she could afford to.

She drives her dream car to an empty house with an empty heart desiring to be loved unconditionally by a strong man. When a man loves this woman, you must have patience and fill her heart with joy that she has searched for in other places and things.

Part of her nourishment is for you to give her full attention. You cannot allow her degrees and salary to intimidate you.

Understand underneath all that stuff is a woman and she is your lover and possibly life partner.

The man who loves this woman must have long suffering with her because in most cases she has acquired a sense of pride that she is more than meets the eye and she is.

But do not allow these assets to confuse the issue at hand, she need a man!

She has attempted to satisfy her ego by taking trips with her best girl friend, (*please watch that best girl friend*), and find happiness in the party life that has not fulfilled her void. She needs a man's love just like any other woman.

Love her and be patient with her until she put the degrees in the closet and pull out the Victoria Secret.

Foreplay and fondling will bring out of her two or three different sensual personalities in the same evening.

When a man captures the heart of this woman she will accept him and drop her sense of pride, haughty spirit and make you king of her heart.

You will know that you are in the house when she introduces you to the best girl friend and call you big daddy in her presence.

Chapter Five

You will know that you have put it down right when she gladly introduces you to her stiff-necked academia peers with a proud smile.

Love this woman and never let her go because she is an asset to your life. Do all you can to offer protection and security to her life and never depend solely on her finances?

Six

Variety of Bones to Suck On!

The Feminine Woman

She is an elegant woman very quiet and compassionate Lady, who sows marital accord.

Her character from the inside elucidates her beauty on the outside. Everybody knows she is a woman because she is secure in her femininity. This woman is easy to love because her elegance covers her flaws.

There is nothing weak about this woman because she is sure of who she is. She walks with a sense of dignity, even crosses her legs with a sense of poise and grace. She stresses interdependence with man and there is no doubt she desires a man.

She endorses cooperation with man and her emphasis is to be the right woman for man. She is refined in the arts; knows how to dine with kings and never lose the common touch.

When a man loves this woman please have a pocket full of money and a heart full of love for her only. Assist her in small matters and always be there to help because underneath all the poise she is clumsy in many ways. She is very passionate in love making, very sensitive and detailed.

She knows what she wants and how to accomplish it, but need your support in her failures. When a man loves this woman, he remains thoroughly furnished for every good work. She desires plenty of it; and is easily pleased.

The Feminist Woman

She is just the opposite from the feminine woman. She sows marital discord and is fooled to masculinize herself into thinking that she does not need a man. She emphasizes dependence

Chapter Six

from man, and that she stands alone without man. She also emphasizes aggressive action against man and she is an arrogant woman.

In corporate America, you will find her trying to usurp authority over man and she strives to be the boss of man.

In some cases, her love life consists of another woman or a weak-kneed low self-esteem pair of pants. She is confused and God is not the author of it.

When a man loves this woman, he must move into her life with intentions on taking full control. She desires to be loved and made love too. But has never had the pleasure and company of a strong man.

The man who loves this woman must use wisdom and make friends with her. Be very vigilant to observe her weakness concerning lovemaking. React very gently upon the least amount of femininity observed.

If she mentions the movies; take her, if she looks at flowers buy them, if she mentions a sport; play it with her or take her to the game.

When a man loves this woman, he should firmly hang with her having long suffering and patience until you bring out all her feminine virtues.

Understand that underneath that entire hard core; she sits down to use the bathroom. Don't allow her to stand up in your face and boss you around. She is the weaker vessel, and she is very much a woman.

After you win her heart and you will know when you have; because she will become very soft like putty in your hand. Some of the hard things she used to say and do will eventually soften up in conversation.

Be very vigilant for this sign, because this is your entrance. She knows you have been patient with her; but will not tolerate her mess.

She has realized that you may be her last man standing. No one desires to miss out on real love.

However, she is still a very optimistic lady who needs full assurance; she is not completely at peace with herself.

When a man loves this woman, he will calm her fears and learn to love her idiosyncratic behaviors.

The Church Girl

> *She is a wonderful person and a marvelous human being.*

She is a woman, a lady, and a girl. She has the same desires as any other human being of the female gender. She loves to be cared for and treated special. She loves to have fun and is full of laughter as any woman.

She is well groomed and possesses a pleasing personality. She loves her pastor and her example usually is the first lady of the church or an older respectful woman.

Usually her desire is for one man because of her Christian upbringing. She is tender hearted and loving. She is aware of unconditional love because of her relationship with the Lord. She now desires paternal love from man in holy matrimony. *They love to eat!*

Usually she is involved in some auxiliary in the church working out her soul salvation; and if she is single her eyes is fixed on the first man who seems to have interest in her. She is looking for her husband relentlessly.

The worst thing a man can do is miss-treat this woman. When mistreating this woman, you are not only hurting a gift from God but also the God in her. The man who loves this woman should have very serious intentions on keeping her for life or don't date her at all.

Some church girls are very insecure because of the hype fed to them in many religious settings that has nothing to do with the moral standing of true religion and the realities of mundane life.

She has been led to believe that her faith will warrant her true felicity all her life but they forgot to include the work.

Chapter Six

You will find her rallying around the first lady of the church and the upcoming programs that benefit the growth of the church, singing in the choir or some other ministry. The single ladies are close to becoming a virtuous woman; all she need is fulfillment in her life and that is her future husband.

Don't play this woman cheap; she is very powerful in her purpose because God has placed it in her. Whenever you cross her path you cross the path of something that God is giving out.

Like everyone else she has some issues but the Lord is working on her daily.

She is a very compassionate and a passionate woman. She desires to be loved and made love too; just as any other woman; she also desires excitement in her life. Church is her life because of her faith but she is a very qualified lover that very much desires the human touch from a man.

The foundation for a great relationship and a great marriage is already set.

The man who loves this woman should follow the Lord and she will follow him. She can be very jealous hearted and in some cases domineering. But do not allow her to dominate anything.

Consider her opinions always, but stand up as a strong man. She understands strength because God is the strength of her life.

When she did not have a man, she depended upon the Lord! The man who loves her must be ready to settle down and sacrifice his life for her.

She doesn't desire to share the love of God in you with another. She has had some bad experiences in the past; just as any other woman, but knows they are under the blood; and expects you to feel the same.

The man that loves this woman must be for real because the anointing on her knows when appointing on you is up to no good. Anointing must meet anointing: then some appointing can come into play.

Although she is the weaker vessel she is strong in the Lord. The man who loves this woman must respect, protect, and spoil her because that's what she is used too by the God who already loves her unconditionally. There is no room for anything else but a great life with the church girl. Just do unto her as God would do, when a man loves this woman.

The Wealthy Woman

Obviously don't have a need for material things. It is God's word and the writer's opinion that happiness is not in the abundance of things. This woman can travel to the uttermost parts of the world, live in the best resorts and eat the finest of foods. She can drive the finest cars, wear the finest clothes and jewels that most of the others mentioned only dream of.

But without love she is homeless in her heart and pitiful in her purpose. If she does not find unconditional love she may become vulnerable and condescend to the level of an alcoholic or an over the counter drug addict. She may become confused and miss-directed in her passion, and attempts to buy love in all the wrong places.

In some cases, her demons have miss-directed her passions and directed her to make sorry attempts at being a socialite but deep down inside her desire is to fulfill her fantasies with one man and be his tramp in the bedroom.

Some men in her arena are too busy to give her the attention she deserves or they are in awe of her wealth. She is very protective of her holdings and justifiably so.

But this woman will give up all for real unconditional love. She has tried everything and I mean everything to find love and the right chemistry in love making with the right man.

This is a very serious case where the man who loves this woman must learn to fall in love with her faults and shortcomings because they are plentiful. When a man loves this woman, he cannot allow her wealth to blind him of her real need; which is sexual healing and unconditional love.

It will take a strong man to love and fulfill the desires of this woman without considering her

Chapter Six

wealth. She has bought her way all her life but you must keep in the forefront of her mind and heart that money can't buy her love; when a man loves this woman.

The more a person has acquired in life the more issues they have in life.

The Treacherous Woman

Is the worst of all women, her motives are always selfish and her agenda hidden with very little concern if any of the pain or ruin she leaves in her path... She has never had any recognition as a lady; so, her stage is raising hell and causing strife wherever she is.

She will say anything out of her mouth anywhere at any time, which emulates from her heart, "For out of the abundance of the heart the mouth speaks." You don't have to look for her just listen to what comes out of her, mostly profanity because of her limited vocabulary.

She thinks nothing of setting you up for a robbery or to get you killed. You'll find her always leaching from others, and following in the shadow of another want to be because she has no identity of her own.

The blind leads the blind. If you will notice her attire, it is not always indicative of her deceit and full intentions. She may have stolen a pair red bottoms, carry a knock off Louie but she will wear house slippers to the mall and the heel of her feet is rusty.

She hates weak men but they are her prey. She has used young boys and men of low self-esteem to feed her habits and vices and she usually carries a body odor. Her focus is a one-track mind, stuck on what she can take to feed her vices, her whisky drinking, weed smoking and cocaine using.

You'll know her because no one in her family associates with her and she doesn't even get along with her mother and father. And the only time she is somewhat nice is when she is trying to maneuver a move for personal gain.

Chapter Six

Deny her one or two times after she puts her beg on and you will see the real person.

Her sex life has consisted of younger men, other women and group orgies. She has experienced every illegal drug on the market and anything over the counter that will give her a buzz.

She is in awe and angry with successful women because she is covetous of what they have.

She's quick tempered, very inpatient and always in other folk business. Being a lady is about as farfetched from her as a monkey driving a Bentley Arnege.

Usually the only man that she respects is the gangster man well versed in street life whose motive is to get a good money run out of her trickery, stealing and prostitution.

There is much more to say about this woman and some of it only God knows. The regular Joe who loves this woman should be versed in demon warfare, and have a constant prayer life before Almighty God.

When she is set free from total bondage she will make someone a strong wife but I wouldn't take the chance. Some things and some people you just give over to God and leave it alone.

The Virtuous Woman

Can be trusted and there is no price that can be paid for her presence in your life. She is a good woman and there is not an evil thought against you all the days of her life.

She is a natural helper and understands her position in caring for the things that concern you.

This fantastic, marvelous gift from above simply recessed from heaven an entered your life. Her joy is learning to fit in every aspect of your life to satisfy you. She will balance your life when you are wrong and bless your life when you are right.

You can depend on her cleanliness, preparing your meals with love at the appropriate times and frugal for the household without fail.

Chapter Six

She is not selfish and always seeking valuables that will enhance your wealth. She is a homemaker with an entrepreneur mind and skills to help pay the bills. You can call her dependent with an interdependent heart.

You will find her giving to the poor; working with her hands in her own strength; relentless tending to the needy. She is well groomed in fine silks, wools and linen and one of her favorite colors is purple.

But don't judge her by her attire, because strength and honor are her clothing. Listen to her speak; you'll find that wisdom flows from her lips like honey and kindness is always in her tongue.

She is not an idle woman and looks out for her household, not allowing her candle to go out because of the night. *She is always available for loves.*

Who can find such a woman?

www.ingramcontent.com/pod-product-compliance
Lightning Source LLC
Chambersburg PA
CBHW070559100426
42744CB00006B/343